Attending the Lord's Table
by Henry Tozer
with chapters by C. Matthew McMahon

Copyright Information

Attending the Lord's Table, by Henry Tozer, with chapters by C. Matthew McMahon
Edited by Therese B. McMahon

Copyright ©2020 by Puritan Publications and A Puritan's Mind

Some language and grammar have been updated from the original manuscript. Any change in wording or punctuation has not changed the intent or meaning of the original author(s), and has been made to aid the modern reader.

Published by Puritan Publications
A Ministry of A Puritan's Mind ®
Crossville, TN
www.puritanpublications.com
www.apuritansmind.com

All rights reserved. No part of this publication may be reproduced, stored in a retrieval system or transmitted in any form by any means, electronic, mechanical, photocopy, recording or otherwise, without the prior permission of the publisher, except as provided by USA copyright law.

Manufactured in the United States of America

eISBN: 978-1-62663-370-4
ISBN: 978-1-62663-371-1

Table of Contents

A Primer on the Supper 4

Meet Henry Tozer 12

Preface 15

Chapter 1: What a Sacrament is and How Many there Are 18

Chapter 2: What is the Lord's Supper? 20

Chapter 3: The Necessity of Receiving the Lord's Supper 25

Chapter 4: The Necessity of Preparation 37

Chapter 5: Concerning Examination in General 40

Chapter 6: The Examination of Our Knowledge 44

Chapter 7: The Examination of Our Repentance 48

Chapter 8: The Examination of Our Faith 57

Chapter 9: The Examination of Our Love 60

Chapter 10: Of Premeditation and Prayer 72

Chapter 11: Meditation at the Lord's Table 78

Chapter 12: Of Practice 85

Other Books on the Lord's Supper 102

A Primer on the Supper
by C. Matthew McMahon, Ph.D., Th.D.

The Lord's Supper is to be *used* in perpetual remembrance for the Christian, unlike baptism which is administered once (though baptism is to be perpetually *remembered* and *improved*). The Lord's Supper is physically *administered* each time the body partakes of it, "as often as you do this..." as a means of grace to those who need grace. What Christian does not need grace? What Christian does not need *more* grace, and that week by week? At what point should the means of grace be used "sparingly" instead of diligently, often, and with striving? One fellow asked me not long ago, "how often should we partake of the Lord's Supper?" My answer to him was, *as much as you may need the means of grace while you live in this world.* Do we sin? Do we need comfort? If we do, the means of grace are quite necessary and ought to be used *often.* In our own church service, we partake of the Lord's Supper every week to take constant advantage of the means of grace.

The supper is used for our instruction because we are quite often and by nature spiritually *weak* and in need of much spiritual help. Jesus instituted something *visible* in the sacraments of both baptism and the Lord's Supper to teach us, and connect, that which we see and experience, to the truth of the reality behind it. Bread signifies the body of Christ. Wine signifies the blood of Christ (Romans 3:25). The very act of taking the elements sets forth Christ to believers. The breaking of the bread represents Christ's death (John 1:12) and the pouring of the wine represents his shed blood. In taking them, we are receiving of the elements signifying receiving Christ. But it is not, as many think, a *mere* remembrance. It is truly a means of grace communicated to faithful believers.

When we partake of the sacrament of the Lord's Supper over and over, we ought to have a solemn engagement to our duty to Christ. We are to be a chaste, faithful and loving spouse to the Bridegroom. We are to reciprocate the love of Christ exhibited in the supper to us, back to him again. In doing this we remember Christ's death on our behalf, and we receive Christ's communion with us (Revelation 3:20). We do this as a church body for the glory of God.

Hebrews 12:29 says, "For our God is a consuming fire." There are two ways "fire" is expressed towards people. To the lost (2 Thess. 1:8), "In flaming fire taking vengeance on them that know not God, and that obey not the Gospel of our Lord Jesus Christ:" That type of fire is a *destroying* fire. Then to the elect, it is a *refining* fire. 1 Peter 1:7 says, "That the trial of your faith, being much more precious than of gold that perisheth, though it be tried with fire." The Lamb was roasted for us. He underwent our fire. When the supper is before us, we must be conscious to do away with all sinful thoughts, knowing the Lamb has been roasted for us. You may come with the bitter herbs of contrition for sin, but you may not come with and in your sins, for that is eating with leavened bread. When we come to eat at the Lord's table, we come to feast on the roasted Lamb (1 Corinthians 5:7–8). This is the cross of Christ as a demonstration in the ultimacy of the wrath of God and the love of God.

Since the death of the Son of God for us is the most important event in the history of salvation, it should be held in *perpetual* remembrance. We should not be thinking about the Lord's Supper we took four months ago. We should be *perpetually* remembering it and breaking break each time we come together, as the early church did (Acts 2:42). It was to this end that our blessed Lord instituted this sacrament, and accompanied the institution with the command, "This do in remembrance of me." In the Lord's Supper the believer receives Christ by faith. He *receives* Christ's body and blood. The Apostle asserts that the bread which we break is a fellowship and participation of the body of Christ, and that the cup which we bless is a participation of the blood of Christ, (*e.g.* 1 Cor. 10:16). It is also important to keep in mind that participation in the sacrament with fellow believers in a covenant community is not optional. Christ said in John 6:53, "Except ye eat the flesh of the Son of man, and drink his blood, ye have no life in you." Christ says to every believing communicant, "This is my body broken *for you*. This is my blood shed *for you*." As a summary of *the 1647 Westminster Confession*, and other Reformed confessions, the Supper may be expressed in this light:

The Lord's Supper is a holy ordinance instituted by Christ; as a memorial of his death, in which, under the symbols of bread and wine, his body as broken and his blood as shed for the remission of sins, are signified, and, by the power of the Holy Spirit, sealed and applied to believers; by which their union with Christ and their mutual fellowship are set forth and confirmed, their faith strengthened, and their souls nourished to eternal life.

Consider that our Lord Jesus, in the night in which he was betrayed, instituted the sacrament of his body and blood, to be observed in his church to the end of the world by his covenant people. He did this for the perpetual remembrance of the sacrifice of himself in his death, the sealing of all its all benefits to true believers, their spiritual nourishment and growth in him, their further engagement in and to all duties which they owe to him; and to be a bond and pledge of their communion with him, and with each other, as members of his mystical body.

At the same time, in thinking about what occurs in the supper, and what grace is received by the sacrament, as Mr. Tozer will faithfully demonstrate, 1 Corinthians 11, which gives us a warning that we must examine ourselves before coming, being sure we are in the faith, that we are not lost, so that we do not eat or drink condemnation on ourselves. "Wherefore whosoever shall eat this bread, and drink this cup of the

Lord, unworthily, shall be guilty of the body and blood of the Lord. But let a man examine himself, and so let him eat of that bread, and drink of that cup. For he that eateth and drinketh unworthily, eateth and drinketh damnation to himself, not discerning the Lord's body."

Tozer will point out the manner and method of coming *rightly* to the Lord's Table, *i.e.* in examination. All Christians are to judge themselves, that they would not be judged of the Lord. They are to consider if they have truly repented for their past sins, and that they have a lively and steadfast faith in Christ their Savior. They are to be seeking salvation only in the merits of Christ's death and passion, always refusing and forgetting all malice and debate, with full purpose to live in brotherly peace and godly conversation all the days of their life.

All those who are worthy receivers, who outwardly partake of the visible elements in the sacrament, inwardly by faith, really and indeed, yet not carnally and corporally, but spiritually, receive and feed on Christ crucified, and all benefits of his death. Christ is really and spiritually present to the faith of believers in this ordinance, as the elements themselves are, to their outward senses.

This holy action, ordained of God, is where the Lord Jesus, by earthly and visible things is set before his people, and it lifts them up to heavenly and invisible things. And that when Jesus had prepared his spiritual banquet, he witnessed that he himself was the bread of life by which the souls of believers are fed to everlasting life.

Therefore, in setting forth bread and wine to eat and drink, Christ confirms and seals up to us his promise and communion (that is, that all believers shall be partakers with him in his Kingdom); and he represents to them, and makes plain to their senses, his heavenly gifts; and also gives to them himself, to be received with faith, and not just with mouth. It is a recollection of that blessed sacrifice that was offered on the cross for our sins; *and* it is a sealing up of all the benefits of our redemption. It is, in fact, an *exhibition* of Jesus Christ. It is a *deed of gift* of the Christ. God goes about giving Christ to his people in it, and all that labor to come worthily before him. This is the pressure that Tozer will bring the reader of this work. To come worthily, in grace, as instructed by the Lord, will cause the communicant great benefits of Christ's grace.

There cannot be a greater feast in which Christ is the gift that is bestowed; Christ is the banquet, yes, Christ and *all* his benefits. And this is given solely through the power of the Holy Spirit, that his people, being fed with his flesh, and refreshed with his blood, may be renewed in their covenant both to true godliness and to immortality.

It is true, due to the heinousness of sin, when his people are all fallen in Adam, they have been engulfed into such a bottomless abyss of misery, that *nothing* but the blood of a God could deliver them. There was an infinite breach by sin between God and his people. This breach could never be made up but by the blood of God. When the bread is broken, it was sin that caused Christ's body to be broken; and when the wine is poured out, it was sin which caused Christ's blood to be poured out. It was for sin and the satisfaction he rendered to God and his righteousness, that caused Christ to suffer so much for his people.

Matthew 26:26-30 says, "And as they were eating, Jesus took bread, and blessed it, and brake it, and gave it to the disciples, and said, Take, eat; this is my body. And he took the cup, and gave thanks, and gave it to them, saying, Drink ye all of it; For this is my blood of the new testament, which is shed for many for the remission of sins. But I say unto you, I will not drink henceforth of this fruit of the vine, until that day when I drink it new with you in my Father's kingdom. And when they had sung an hymn, they went out into the mount of Olives." When Christians take of the bread, they ought to remember and believe that the body of the Lord Jesus Christ was given for a complete remission of all their sins. When they take of the cup, they are to remember and believe that the precious blood of the Lord Jesus Christ was shed for a complete remission of all their sins. And then, they must never believe that they have done their duty when they have merely *received* the Lord's Supper. It would signify but little, if after preparing for the supper, examining themselves in light of the supper, receiving the supper, and going their way after the supper, that they do not cast away all sin. To cast off sin, is both a preparative for the Lord's Supper, and must be its consequence, as Tozer will faithfully show. He will guide the reader in understanding the meaning of the supper, how to prepare for the supper, what examination in light of the supper means, what to examine (our knowledge, repentance, faith and love), what to consider during the supper, and how to practice and live after we have partaken of the supper.

May all God's people live in a worthy manner befitting what they do in participating in this ordinance of the Christ.

In Christ's grace,
C. Matthew McMahon, Ph.D., Th.D.
From my study, November, 2020.

Meet Henry Tozer
by C. Matthew McMahon, Ph.D., Th.D.

Henry Tozer (1602-1650) was a puritan royalist, born in 1602 at North Tawton, Devonshire. He attended Exeter College, Oxford, beginning in May 3, 1621, and graduated with a B.A. on June 18, 1623. Three years later, he earned his M.A. on April 28, 1626. Having entered, into the ministerial office to preach the Gospel, it is said, that he was useful in moderating, reading to novices, and lecturing in the chapel.[1] He was appointed the lecturer at St. Martin's Church (Carfax, Oxford) on October 21, 1632, and proceeded to earn his B.D. on July 28, 1636. He was an able and a laborious preacher, had a great amount of the primitive religion in his sermons; and seemed to be a most precise puritan in his demeaner and life, on which account his sermons and expositions in the churches of St. Giles and St. Martin in Oxford, were always attended by the puritanical party. He held puritan views, and elected in 1643 to the Westminster Assembly, but did not attend the assembly in order to remain at Oxford and preach before the king. Tozer was a noted theologian, and having preached at Christ's Church before his majesty, or at St. Mary's before the parliament, he was appointed by the chancellor of the university, in 1646, to take his doctor's degree; but this he refused. He was appointed minister at Yarnton in

---

[1] Brook, Benjamin, *The Lives of the Puritans*, vol. 3 (London: James Black, 1813), 112–113.

1644. He probably served the church from the city of Oxford, as he never lived in Yarnton.

As sub-rector of Exeter College, Tozer managed the college in the absence of George Hakewill, the rector. In March 1647 he was cited before the parliamentary visitors for continuing the common prayer, and for his known disfavor to parliamentarians. In November he was summoned to Westminster before the parliamentary commission, and the following year was imprisoned for some days on refusing to give up the college books. He was expelled from his fellowship on May 26, 1648, and on June 4 was ejected from St. Martin's Church by soldiers because he prayed for the king, and "breathed out pestilent air of unsound doctrine." The decree, however, was revoked on November 2, and Tozer was allowed to travel for three years, retaining his room in Exeter College.

Tozer then went to Holland, and became minister to the English merchants at Rotterdam, where he died on September 11, 1650; he was buried in the English church there. Dr. Thomas Marshall, who succeeded him in the preacher's office, says, "he was always taken for an honest and a conscientious puritan."[2]

He was author of the following works, all published at Oxford:

---

[2] Wood's *Athenæ Oxon.* vol. i. p. 72. And, *Biog. Britan.* vol. vi. p. 4076.

1. "Directions for a Godly Life," dedicated to his pupil Lorenzo Cary, son of Viscount Falkland,' 1628, 16mo, 5th ed. 1640, 8th 1671, 10th 1680, 11th 1690, 13th 1706 12mo.
2. "A Christian Amendment," 1633.
3. "Christus: sive Dicta Facta Christi," 1634.
4. "Christian Wisdom," 1639, 12mo.

For further study:

Foster's Alumni Oxon. 1500-1714; Wood's *Athenae*, ed. Bliss, iii. 273, and *Hist. and Antiq. Univ. Oxford*, vol. ii.pt. ii, pp. 508, 531, 552-4, 574, 588, 590, 593, 594; Wood's *Life and Times*, i. 444, and *Hist. of Kidlington*, pp. 220, 222, 223, *etc.*, both published by Oxford Hist. Soc.; Prince's *Worthies of Devon*, p. 574; *Hist. MSS. Cornm.* 2nd Rep. App. p. 127; Cal. *State Papers*, Dom. 1629-31, p. 260; Boase's *Register of Exeter Coll.* pp. cix, cxvii-cxx, 99; Conant's *Life*, p. 9; Madan's *Early Oxford Press*; Walker's *Sufferings*, ii. 115; Brook's *Lives of the Puritans*, iii. 112; *Journals of the House of Commons*, ii. 541.

Preface

To the honorable Gentleman Mr. Lorenzo Cary, Son to the Right Honorable Vicount Faulkland Lord Deputy of Ireland.

Worthy Sir,

    Since the time that it first pleased your honorable father to commend you to the religious government of this college, with this you now live, your carriage has been so sweet and lovely, that it has won, I dare say, the heart of each member of it to a readiness of respecting your goodness, as in word so in deed, according to their several places and dignities. Neither could I suffer myself, standing in a more near relation than any of the rest to you, to come short in the performance of this office. To this, I here offer to your religious meditation this ensuing *treatise*, collected and composed first for private use, but now published. This is not to gain the applause of any (from which my own unworthiness sufficiently checks me) but chiefly for these two respects: first to testify that love, which I both owe to you and am ready to make good. Secondly and more principally, to invite you to a due consideration of those holy duties in it contained, that by a seasonable knowledge of these things contained in it your actions may be more carefully ordered, and God's name in the faithful practice of it may be more fully glorified.

The subject is a matter not of human learning, but of God's service; and of it a part, without exception, the greatest. It concerns the right receiving of Holy Communion. This is a duty, I confess, better known, then well considered; and more often thought on, then sincerely practiced. If it were not so, bad actions would not be so commonly privileged by the greatness of the agents, as now they are; but they to whom God has given most honor here, would ever think it their greatest glory to honor him most again by their faithful service to him. And there is a good reason why they should, for if they remember to whom God has given most, of them he requires most again. Yes, such who have the precedency of others in place and dignity, may do well to consider that in making a conscience of matters of religion and leading their lives according to its rules, they do not only provide well for the salvation of their own souls, but give a good occasion to others also. They happily provoke them to practice the same duties by their good examples. These examples are ever held as lively precepts, and serve for a secret reproof to an ingenuous inferior, when he shall see himself defective in in this where his betters have gone before him.

Let the honorable and mighty in this way remember how far they shall honor God by a religious life, and then they cannot but acknowledge that it is their glorious freedom to be his humble servants. Others, if they please, may take notice of this persuasion; and perhaps they would, if I were not unworthy to advise them. But now I speak to you alone, whom I well know is willing as freely to make use of others help so truly to accept of this from me. Your own happiness you must confess, with thanks to God, that by his providence you live in that society, whose religion is as firm as undefiled. Where you cannot say you lack the rule either of loving precepts or example according to which you have already joined with the rest in a religious communicating at the Lord's Table. My desire is to persuade you to a constant perseverance in what you have so well begun; that so devoting your tender years, with those which follow to the service of the Almighty, you may again from him receive and fully enjoy his daily blessing, which always attends on those that truly seek him. Some meditations which perhaps may serve for your direction, I here present to your view; in which I freely acknowledge almost nothing is mine (to prevent the censure of a curious reader) but only the labor of composing. This I now commend to you, and you to the blessed providence of the most Highest, resting ever *as:*

Yours truly in the Lord
HENRY TOZER

Chapter 1:
What a Sacrament is and How Many there Are

A sacrament is an outward visible sign of an inward and invisible grace. It is ordained by God, by which he seals to us his Covenant of Grace made in the blood of Christ, and we again testify of our faith and piety towards him in it. So that it is both a sign in respect of the thing signified, and a seal in respect of the covenant by which it is sealed to us. The word *sacrament* properly signifies an oath, by which soldiers bound themselves to their general. It is taken from here to signify that obligation by which we tie ourselves to the blessed and sweet service of Jesus Christ. For by this we, as Christ's soldiers, first bind ourselves by promise of obedience to fight under the Lord's banner against the world, the flesh and the devil. Then also, secondly, we put on the cognizance and arms, the colors and mark of Christ by professing our faith in him, so that it may appear to the world to whom we do belong.

Now sacraments are of two sorts. First of the Old Testament, which were two. First circumcision, secondly the Passover. The first was ordained for a sign of entrance into the covenant; the second for an assurance of confirmation of, and continuance in the same. Both which are now abolished, and instead of them we now have the sacraments of the New

Testament, which are also two. First baptism answerable to circumcision; secondly the Lord's Supper to the Passover. Both are signified by that water and blood which issued out of the side of Christ, when it was pierced by the soldiers on the cross. Of these the first is called the sacrament of our nativity or entrance, because by it we are assured that we are received into the Covenant of Grace, and so are regenerate and belong to the flock of Christ. The second is called the sacrament of our growth and perseverance, by which we grow up in Christ, and are assured that we shall be still kept in this estate. So that both are necessary; the one to assure us of our entrance into, and the other of our continuance in the estate of grace. For although that grace once conferred cannot be lost, yet our assurance often lacks strengthening by reason of our manifold temptations. Against these we are comforted by the remembrance of Christ's death and passion. This also teaches us why the sacrament of baptism is received but once, and the Lord's Supper often. This is because our birth is signified by our baptism, and we can be born but once. But, we daily stand in need of food and strengthening, and so we often receive the supper of the Lord, that our souls may be nourished to life everlasting.

Chapter 2:
What is the Lord's Supper?

That we may rightly understand the sacrament of the Lord's Supper we must know two things: 1. What it is, and 2. What belongs to its due receiving.

For the first; the Lord's Supper is a sacrament, consisting of bread and wine lawfully consecrated and distributed; instituted by Christ himself for a continual remembrance of the death and passion of Christ, and the benefits which we receive by it.

This institution was at Christ's last supper after he had eaten the Passover with his disciples; so that it is called *a supper* in respect of the time of the institution; and the Lord's Supper in respect of the author, the Lord Christ. We also use this designation in respect to its end, which is partly to set forth the Lord's death, and the spiritual food in it received, namely the body and blood of Christ himself.

In this sacrament we must consider two things: 1. The parts, and, 2. The end.

There are two parts. First, the outward signs, and then secondly, the thing signified. The signs are either representing, namely the elements themselves, or applying signs, which are the actions about those elements.

There are two elements. Bread and wine; not only bread, but both, according to Christ's institution. And this is not the bread dipped in the wine, as some will have it; because Christ's blood was shed out of his body for our sins, and we are to receive these signs as representing Christ, not whole but wounded and pierced.

Now Christ chose those elements before any other, because they best serve to set forth Christ's body and blood; for as bread by diverse breakings and pressings comes to be perfect, yes, the chiefest, food of our bodies, still giving a good relish when other things do not, and is also more common to all than any other. So the body of Christ by many torments was made the chief nourishment of our souls, remaining always most sweet and pleasant, and common to all that can receive him by faith. And as wine cherishes and comforts us, satisfies our thirst, purges away many corrupt desires, and makes us bold and adventurous, so the blood of Christ revives and gladdens our drooping souls, satisfies our spiritual thirst, purges us from all our sins, and makes us courageous against all fear of our enemy, the devil. Again, as bread is made of many grains into one loaf, and wine of many grapes into one cup, so we, partaking of it, and of Christ, by faith, are made one with him as our Head, and also one among ourselves as members of his body. So much for the elements.

The actions in this sacrament are of two sorts. 1. Of the minister, and, 2. Of the communicants. The actions of the minister are these. 1. Setting apart, and 2. Blessing of the elements, by which is signified that Christ Jesus was set apart and sanctified for us, as it is said, "And for their sakes I sanctify myself, that they also might be sanctified through the truth," (John 17:19). 3. Breaking and pouring out, and 4. Distributing to the communicants; by which is signified that Christ's body was crucified and his blood shed, and that its benefits are offered to us, *if* we have faith to receive them, as it is shown in John 3:15. He was lifted up, "that whosoever believeth in him should have life everlasting."

The actions of the communicants are two. 1. Taking, and, 2. Eating and drinking. By which is signified that they, which receive benefit by Christ, must receive him by faith applying his merits to their own souls, "But as many as received him, to them gave he power to become the sons of God, even to them that believe on his name," (John 1:12).

In this way, you have the signs and the thing signified which is the body and blood of Christ, with the benefits, which we receive by it. These benefits are, namely, the strengthening and refreshing of our souls in the remission of our sins. And this we receive, not of the minister (for he only gives the signs) but of God himself, apprehending the same by our faith. For Christ is not signified in these signs as in a picture, but exhibited to us, being himself present in the sacrament, though not corporally to the bread and wine. He is there spiritually to our faith. For his body is in heaven and must remain there until the last day, as it is Acts 3:2. Yet, we may feed on him spiritually by faith by applying his death and passion to our sinful souls. So that there is one union between Christ and the elements, which is symbolic, and another between Christ and us, which is spiritual and real.

The ends of this sacrament are twofold: 1. In respect of others, and 2. In respect of ourselves.

In respect of others, it testifies to them the faith which we profess; they see our readiness in this and may have their hearts also stirred up to such good duties. In respect of ourselves it concerns either what we have received from, or what we are to return to God. In the first respect it serves, first for remembrance; namely, of the death of Christ; for, "as often as we receive this, we show the Lord's death till he come," (1 Cor. 11:26).

Secondly, for confirmation to us; and that, both of our union among ourselves, as in 1 Cor. 10:17, "For we being many, are one bread and one body, for we all partake of one bread," as also of our communion with Christ. For as the bread and wine are turned into the substance of our bodies; so we by faith are united unto Christ, and made flesh of his flesh, "for his flesh is meat indeed, and his blood is drink indeed," (John 6.55). For this cause it is called *communion*.

In the second respect concerning that which we are to return to God, it serves to testify our thankfulness to God for his mercy in giving us his Son, and in him all things. In it he is assuring us by this seal. We cannot but remember him when we consider the torments that he endured for our sins, which were indeed the very nails and spears that pierced him. And for this cause it is called the *Eucharist*, because in it we offer up *our thanks* to God. It may also be called a sacrifice. It is not a sacrifice in that we in it offer up Christ to God, (for Christ himself at once finished this offering of his body on the cross), but because we offer up our thankful hearts to God for his mercy in Christ, so that it is a sacrifice, not of Christ, but of our thankfulness.

Chapter 3:
The Necessity of Receiving the Lord's Supper

That we may receive this sacrament, as we ought, we must consider two things: 1. The necessity, and, 2. The right manner of receiving it. As for the first, we must know that it is not an indifferent thing for us to receive or not to receive at our pleasure, but that we ought to do it though not every sabbath after the custom observed in the primitive church, yet without fail, as often as occasion is offered; according to the example of those in the acts, who continued steadfast in breaking of bread, (Acts 2:42).[3]

The necessity of which duty will further appear, if we consider these two things: 1. The principal cause, which often keeps us from it; and, 2. The motives, which may draw us to it.

First, that, which makes us backward in its performance, is without question the policy of our arch-enemy, the devil. He strives by all means to draw us away, either by a careless neglect of our chiefest good to feed rather on our own foolish imaginations (as he

---

[3] Tozer does not give any biblical reason that the Lord's Supper ought not to be taken weekly, and implies that the primitive church took it weekly (who continued steadfast in that way). To say one thing and then the other is contradictory to sound practice if one is to partake of the supper "as often as occasion is offered" as he says. – Ed.

mentioned those in the Gospel narrative where those who had rather see their ground, or prove their oxen, than taste of that supper to which they were invited in Luke 14:18-19), or else by a nervous fearfulness of our own unworthiness to approach to such a holy banquet as this is. And truly, if we could but see that this is the devil's doing, we would by all means strive against his temptations. For, who among us would not endeavor to the utmost, so far to resist his temporal enemy, as that he should not be able to hurt him either in body or in goods? And shall we be more careful for the preservation of our earthly bodies, then of our heavenly souls, which Christ Jesus has redeemed by his precious blood? God forbid. We must know that God expects more at our hands, and that our souls are never so safe, as when they are in greatest opposition, and do that which is most displeasing to our chiefest enemy, the devil. For the more we please him, the less we please God; and the nearer we are to him, the farther we are from God.

The motives which may draw us to the performance of this duty, are taken from a due consideration of these two things. 1. Who it is which invites us to it, and, 2. What are the consequences of receiving or not receiving the supper.

He which invites us, is God himself, whose ordinance it is; and who requires it at our hands as a principal part of his service. Therefore, as often as we omit it, we may be sure that we offend him. He himself has testified in threatening to cut off that soul from his people, which should forbear to keep the Passover, (Num. 9:13). And if this is so, then doubtless the neglect of this sacrament, where Christ is so fully exhibited to us, is very displeasing to him. He also expresses this in the parable of the great supper, (Luke 14:24), where he says, "None of those men, which were bidden, shall taste of my supper." Why? Because they did not come when they were invited; and if we refuse to come when the Lord calls, who knows whether he will give us life until the next invitation? Let us, therefore, take the Lord's offer, while it is today, unless we end up being cut off before tomorrow.

The next motive is taken from the consequences, and that of not receiving. If we do not receive, we offer a twofold injury; the one to Christ, the other, to ourselves.

To Christ this is seen in two ways. 1. In condemning his ordinance, who commanded his disciples to receive it, (1 Cor. 11:24), and in them it is directed to us. And, 2. In neglecting his love towards us; who (as a father on his deathbed) in the night that he was betrayed, bequeathed this seal and pledge of his love to us. This should be very dear to us, and *at no time* neglected when it is offered.

Again, if we do not receive it, we injure ourselves; and that also in two ways. 1. In respect of our name and profession; for, if we do not come when others do, we expose ourselves to their censure, showing that we are at least neglecters, if not condemners of God's ordinance, who will have *all* to come to it, (Matt. 26:27).

Yes, we show that we do not have the life of a Christian in us, "for whosoever eateth not the flesh of the son of man, and drinketh his blood, hath no life in him," (John 6:53). 2. We injure ourselves from the benefits of it. For, the remembrance of Christ's death and passion (if duly considered) cannot but be a great comfort to us. When we do not take it, we put it from us, as often as we omit the Lord's Supper. And so much we may assure ourselves, that the devil will be ready to take the least occasion to suggest other meditations to us. And it is a miserable thing for us to be exercised in our own pleasures or such likes, when others, with whom we are bound to be present, are reverently gathered together, to the comfort of their own souls, to feed at the Lord's Table? If we say that we are then exercised in other good duties, as reading the word of God or such things, we must know that such duties (good in themselves) are not acceptable to God at such times; and who knows, seeing that in this we neglect the Lord's ordinance, how far God will give the devil leave to tempt us, and draw us away even from those duties to wicked imaginations.

2. The consequences of receiving cannot but invite us to a constant performance of this duty. Now, these consequences respect either God, or ourselves. That which respects God, is our duty of thankfulness and praise, which in this we offer to him for his mercy; which is very pleasant to him, and necessary to be performed of us. This is because he is gracious, and his mercy "endureth forever" towards them that fear him.

And how then can we but with David, have our hearts ready to sing and praise him with the best members that we have? "O God, my heart is fixed; I will sing and give praise, even with my glory," (Psa. 108:1).

That, which respects ourselves, is the benefit which we receive by it; which is twofold. 1. General. 2. More special. The general benefits, which we receive by the Lord's Supper, are chiefly two. 1. A supply of all our needs; which we shall be sure to have if we receive correctly, for the one who "eateth the flesh of Christ, shall never hunger; and he, which drinketh his blood, shall never thirst," as Christ himself has promised. We do not need to doubt of the truth of this, for, he is full of grace and truth, (John 1:14), and in him dwells all fulness, (Col. 1:19). So how then can we lack anything, if we possess him that has all things?

2. It is also an excellent rule to our whole life; for when we by this consider God's great love to us, we cannot (if there is any love and fear of God in us) but be careful to avoid anything, which may be displeasing to him. So that, by this our bodies are made more obedient to our souls, and our souls to God.

The special benefit, which we receive by the Lord's Supper, is in regard of our faith; and this again respects either ourselves and others, or else ourselves alone.

The first is, a testifying of our faith to others; for by this we both show to others the faith, which we profess; and also by our example stir them up to the performance of the same duty. In this respect, therefore, it is necessary that we should often receive it.

In the second respect it is a confirmation and increase of that faith, which we have in us. In this we are to endeavor by all means to continue, as Paul taught the disciples, (Acts 14:22),[4] and beware that we "fall not from our steadfastness, but grow in grace, and in the knowledge of our Lord and Savior Jesus Christ," (2 Peter 3:18). Of this we cannot but be careful, if we consider our weakness; for we are ever subject to apostasy, and our faith is exceedingly weak. We plainly see this by our coldness in prayer and other good duties, by our fear of death, and by our love of this world. For, the strengthening of these things Christ has left to us in this sacrament, as a special means conducing us to overcome those sins. The covenant which our faith takes hold of, as it is contained in the word of God, so it is sealed to us by this sacrament. Therefore, Christ calls the cup, the cup of the *New Testament*, because it seals to us the covenant of God in the New Testament, accomplished in the shedding of Christ's blood. Now if a king should in pity and compassion send a pardon under his seal to a poor distressed prisoner, would we not judge that prisoner unworthy of its benefits, if he should either willfully refuse it, or carelessly neglect it? It is, without question, we would. Yet, such is our case before God,

---

[4] "Confirming the souls of the disciples, and exhorting them to continue in the faith, and that we must through much tribulation enter into the kingdom of God," (Acts 14:22).

who, as king of kings, has sealed to us by this sacrament a full remission of all our sins. If we shall either willfully condemn, or at our pleasure receive this pledge of his love, what can we expect at God's hands, but a just removal of this his favor from us? Surely if we join the consideration of our own weakness, which so much needs help, with the meditation of God's mercy, who so freely gives it, we cannot but acknowledge our own misery if we neglect it. It is here that we fear him, and tender the good of our own souls, so let us be careful in the due performance of this so weighty a business.

Even in light of this, many are accustomed to frame the following excuses for their absence to the supper:

1. The receiving of this sacrament often may breed a disesteem of it; and, therefore, it is safer sometimes to abstain. To this I answer, that in matters temporal (as pleasures, and such like) the often use of them may breed contempt, or at least neglect, as it often does. But, in spiritual things it rather breeds a greater desire, because the more we feel and know their goodness, the more we seek after them. Yet, if it so come to pass, that by often receiving, we begin to undervalue its worth, we must consider that this neglect does not arise from the often use of the thing, but from our corrupt nature. For this exercise is God's own ordinance; always attended with his blessing, if rightly received. It is appointed as a means to stir up and increase our zeal and devotion, and it is not likely that it

should hinder it. Do not let this keep us from the Lord's table, but let us rather come, that it may be a means to increase our piety.

2. Some will say; I am not prepared, and therefore dare not come. But this indeed is no excuse; for we must know that we ought to be always prepared. Our whole life should be a continual preparation, as to all other good duties, so especially to this. We should be ever ready when the Lord shall call, as our Savior admonishes us, (Matt. 24:44).

3. Others will urge, I am to take a journey, or to be employed in such or such a business; and therefore, I cannot come. Well, if this journey or things like it, must of necessity be performed, your excuse is safer. But, if it may be in any way avoided (as oftentimes it may) assure yourself, this is to prefer your own pleasure before that which God commands. A day will certainly come, in this we must give an account for the neglect of the least of God's ordinances; and then it will be said of such pretenses, "who required these things at thy hands?"

4. Some are accustomed to urge; I am not in a loving mood, by reason of some wrong which has been offered to me, and I ought not to come. This indeed is an excuse which is too common. But we must know, that if we are not in a loving frame, it is our own fault; for we ought to be in charity, and still to preserve it. And certainly it is a miserable thing, that we should prefer to feed on our own malice rather than to eat of the Lord's

Supper. This is to hurt ourselves more than we need, even to wrong ourselves because others have wronged us. We should rather seek all means of reconciliation, so that we may remove those impediments of piety and religion, and come more freely to the Lord's table.

5. Some in this way plead for their absence: I am afraid to approach to the Lord's table by reason of my manifold infirmities, which are in me, and therefore I had rather sometimes to refrain, lest I come unworthily, which is a very fearful thing. It is so indeed, but we must consider, that our staying away is no comfort to us in this case, but rather a means to make us worse, and to pull down God's judgments on us. We should rather remember the goodness of God, that invites us, promising to refresh those that are heavy laden with their sins, (Matt. 11:28), not putting us off for our infirmities. For, if there be a willing mind, he accepts us according to that which we have, and not according to that which we do not have, (2 Cor. 8:12), though we lack that perfection, which others have. Yet, if we have a true desire to be refreshed by the merits of Christ, and have a sincere heart before God, he will accept us according to this. Whenever the devil shall tempt you to draw you away by the consideration of your own infirmity, cheer yourself up with the comfort of the blind man in the Gospel. Mark 10:49, "Be of good comfort, behold he calleth thee." Say to yourself, "Christ Jesus has invited me; and has promised to accept me, if my heart is sincere,

humble, and willing; why then should the consideration of my infirmities keep me from it?"

6. Others thus reply: I desire to receive, but I am conscious to myself of some crying sins which I have committed before God, for which I have not yet sufficiently repented. And how then can I partake of this holy banquet in the presence of God? Is it so? Are you poor, and yet will you refuse gold when it is offered to you? Who will you pity for your poverty? Are you desperately sick, and will you not seek the Physician for means of recovery? Who will then bemoan you for your disease? Behold, Christ Jesus is the Physician of your soul, as well able to heal it of all its diseases, as he did the bodies of those, which came to him of their infirmities. Do not forsake this heavenly Physician, but labor by a serious repentance to discharge your conscience of your sins, and then come speedily to him. It is the counsel of the apostle in 1 Cor. 11, who bids us to examine, and then eat. He does not say to us to go away. He says first examine, then eat of this bread and drink of this cup. If you say, I had rather stay away until the next opportunity, that I may have more time to repent. Consider, that the longer you stay away the more sins you will run into, and then it will be so much harder to repent as you ought. And besides that, how do you know whether God will give you grace and time to repent then or not? He has promised indeed to have mercy on a sinner at whatever time he shall repent. But he has not promised to give him grace to repent whenever he wants

to. Seek the Lord while he offers himself to you, that you may find mercy when you seek it.

Lastly, some in a proud manner in this way excuse, (or rather justify) their absence. I do already sufficiently believe whatsoever is proposed in the word of God; and therefore, what need do I have to receive this sacrament so often, as a seal to confirm my faith? It does not in any way confer grace to me; and my faith is so firm, that I persuade myself that I do not need a seal to strengthen it, so much as others do, whose faith is weaker. Therefore, I think that I may sometimes forbear it. But know, Oh vain man, which in this way disputes with your God, that this is God's ordinance, a principal part of his service. This should be diligently performed, even if it in no way profits us, because God had commanded it. Yes, when we have done all those things which are commanded us, we must say that we are unprofitable servants, "we have done but that which was our duty to do," (Luke 17:10). Besides, is your faith so strong that it needs no further strengthening? Do you not perceive daily your weakness of understanding in matters of piety and religion? Is there a frailty in your memory, and a continual disorder in your affections? If not, know this much, that it is a misery to lack this, but a greater misery not to be sensible of our needs. And also know for a certain truth, that when you find in yourself either none, or at least, a small desire of hearing God's word and receiving the sacraments, know, I say, that there is surely some sin or other which is not well repented of. It cloaks your soul, so that your soul cannot delight in those spiritual exercises. Let us, therefore, endeavor to come to the Lord's table as often as we are invited; and when we do come, let us take heed that we do not come for fashion's sake, or to please men, or in any opinion of our own merit in this action. For doing that is not a celebration, but a profanation of the Lord's ordinance, because in this we do not serve God but ourselves. This is a fearful thing, for God is not as man, that he should be deceived. He does not see as man sees. For man judges only according to the outward appearance, but God searches the very heart and reins. He will one day as certainly punish the profaners of his ordinance, as its condemners. Therefore, as we ought in the first place to be fully persuaded of the necessity; so should we in the second by all means labor to come to the knowledge of the right manner of receiving; which is the next thing to be considered.

Chapter 4:
The Necessity of Preparation

He which desires to receive at the Lord's table in a right manner, must be conscience of three duties which are to be performed necessarily. 1. A diligent preparation before partaking. 2. A seasonable meditation in the time of receiving. 3. A religious practice after receiving it in our lives and conversations.

In the first (as before in the matter of receiving) we must take notice of two things. First, the necessity. 2. The right manner of preparation.

The necessity will plainly appear if we consider these two things. 1. In whose presence it is that we are to receive. 2. The danger which we bring on ourselves by not being prepared.

As for the first, we are to feed in the presence of the Lord himself. Now if any, even the best of us, should be invited by a king to his princely table, he would be careful to present himself (if he has a reverence to his presence) in the best manner that he could, putting on then especially (if he have any better than other) his best apparel, and disposing all things in the most decent order, so that he might be better accepted. If this is so, then with what fear and reverence should we then approach the table of this King of kings when he invites us? He stands there ready attended with his angels to behold those, which present themselves, and will soon spy out that man, who shall dare to approach before him, not having on his wedding garment. And what can such a person expect, but, with the man in the Gospel, a casting out into utter darkness? (Matt. 22:12). Neither must we think to deceive the Lord with a hypocritical outward work; for he does not only look not to the outward gesture, but to the inward parts of the soul. It is not so much a clean hand or curious attire which makes us accepted of God, as a pure heart and a cleansed soul, adorned with faith and repentance. We may for a time deceive mortal men, such as ourselves. But when the secrets of our hearts shall be made manifest, then shall our hypocrisy, as well as our negligence, be laid open to our destruction. Let us therefore humble ourselves before God, and prepare ourselves correctly, that we may escape the danger which will otherwise fall on us; which is the second thing to be considered in the necessity of preparation. The danger of not being prepared is particularly set forth to us by considering the offence, which we in this commit, and its reward.

If we come unprepared, and so receive unworthily, our offence is no less than to be guilty of the body and blood of Christ. As Paul says in 1 Cor. 11:27, that is, we offer special disgrace and indignity to Christ, in not receiving him with that reverence which we ought. This offence, as it is in itself very heinous so it draws on us a fearful punishment. The prophet Jeremiah has pronounced him accursed which "doeth the work of the Lord deceitfully," (Jer. 48:10). And if it is so in other things, which are of less importance, what can we expect for the abusing of this weighty matter of the Lord's Supper? The apostle sets down at full the fearfulness of it when he says in 1 Cor. 11:29, "That he, which eateth and drinketh unworthily, eateth and drinketh his own damnation." What can be more terrible than this? Neither is the scripture silent in showing us the judgements of God on such offenders; as we may plainly see, both in the Old Testament, in the sudden death of Uzzah for his rash touching of the ark; and also in the New Testament, in the binding hand and foot for lack of having the wedding garment on. Therefore, let the danger of this move us to a careful preparation, before we presume to come to the Lord's table.

But some may say, I persuade myself, that I can by no means be worthy to receive this sacrament, and how then can I receive worthily? It is true, if we truly consider our own unworthiness and the excellency of this sacrament, we cannot by any means become worthy of it. But this must be our comfort, that he is truly worthy whom God in mercy accepts as worthy; and so he will accept us if we come to him in humility and reverence. Let us therefore, according to the apostle's rule, first try and examine ourselves, and then eat of this supper. Which, that we may the better do, we ought in the next place to take notice of the right manner of preparation.

Chapter 5:
Concerning Examination in General

For our better performance of the duty of preparation, we must be careful to set aside a convenient time before the communion, in laying aside all other impediments. We ought seriously to be exercised in three duties. 1. A diligent examination of our fitness and worthiness to receive. 2. A comfortable premeditation of the benefits, which we are to receive. 3. Earnest prayer to God for a blessing on our endeavors; so that we may be accepted to receive those benefits.

In our examination we are to consider; 1. To whom this duty belongs. And, 2. How it is to be performed.

The first we learn from Paul in 1 Cor. 11, who tells every man to try and examine himself, so that we ourselves are to examine ourselves. Indeed, the ministers of the word of God, and all such, to whom God has committed the charge and care of others, ought carefully to try and examine those, which belong to them. So that, they may be more fit. And inferiors ought also willingly to submit themselves to their trial; yes, if it is not offered, to seek their help when they doubt of anything so that by their directions they may more cheerfully go on. These are duties, which God requires at the hands of everyone; the neglect of this will one day fall heavy on those, which shall fail in the due performance of these things. Yet this is not sufficient; for we are, for the most part, full of hypocrisy, ready to hide our sins from others; yes, we are so clever in iniquity, that we can behave ourselves so smoothly, in respect of the outward show, that others shall find no fault in us at all. And this is in the light, though notwithstanding, that our consciences all the while accuse us of some sins lurking within us. Therefore, we are commanded also to try and examine ourselves in particular.

This examination must be twofold: 1. General, and 2. particular. In the first we must examine ourselves in these two things. 1. Whether we are in the number of the faithful or not; which is very needful to be considered, otherwise we partake in vain. For, as our bodies can receive no nourishing and strengthening from the food, which we daily receive, unless they have some life in them beforehand, so neither can our souls, if they are void of the life of grace. They cannot receive any comfort by this spiritual food in the Lord's Supper. This supper continues and increases life, where it finds it, but works in no one where there is no life before. Let us, therefore, in the first place, diligently try whether Christ is in us or not; of which we shall the more fully assure ourselves, if we can find this persuasion in us, that we (as our forefathers were) are strangers and pilgrims here, Heb. 11:13, looking for a city (as Abraham did) which "hath foundations, whose builder and maker is God." Let us see if we are made free from the bondage of sin by the

Son of God, Christ Jesus, (John 8:36). And so with David, put our whole trust and rely only on his mercy, (Psa. 52:9).

2. We are to make a trial of our readiness, whether we are willing and have a desire to partake of the Lord's Supper or not. God required a willing mind of those which offered anything for building the tabernacle, as it is seen in Exod. 25:2, and also of those which offered him any burnt offerings, (Lev. 19:5). If it is true in these things, which were but shadows of things to come, much more does he expect it at our hands in the performance of this duty, which is the substance itself. Neither yet let us here deceive ourselves, thinking that a bare consent or willing mind is sufficient; it is an hungry desire and appetite, as well as a willingness, to receive meat offered. Yes, that especially, which testifies of a good disposition in the stomach. And God requires in all his service (therefore in this also) that we serve him with all our heart, and with all our soul, (Deut. 10:12). And Christ says, "blessed are they, which hunger and thirst after righteousness, for they shall be filled," (Matt. 5:6). For it is lack of this desire, that many, when they come to the Lord's table, are never the better; because God, as he invites, so he feeds none but those that hunger and thirst, (Isaiah 55:1). Let us therefore try and examine ourselves whether we can say with David, Psalm 42:1, "Like as the hart desireth the water brooks; so longeth my soul after thee, Oh God: my soul is a thirst for God, yes even for the living God. When shall I come to appear

before the presence of God?" If we can find this desire in us, then we are happy. If not, let us humble ourselves before God, and look to him to work and stir up in us the good motions of his Spirit, so that we may attain to some measure of this thirst; and from that go on further to a particular examination of our fitness to receive.

Chapter 6:
The Examination of Our Knowledge

In our particular examination, because we are dull and ignorant in matters, that concern our salvation, and also have, and do often offend both God and our neighbors, all which are hinderances to the due performance of this duty, we must examine ourselves in those particulars which concern both our information in matters which we should understand, as well as our reconciliation with those whom we have offended.

That, which concerns our information, is a good and wholesome knowledge of those things, which God has revealed to us. These things are so necessary, that it is the very ground of all our service of God. For, how can we do the will of God rightly, if we do not know it? Surely any soul that is without knowledge, it is not a good thing, Solomon says in Prov. 19:2. And, therefore, God will have "all men to come to the knowledge of the truth," (1 Tim. 2:6). Without truth can we reap? No, there will be no comfort to ourselves in anything that we do; but we will be as dead men. For, this (and this alone) is life eternal, "that we know God and Jesus Christ whom he hath sent," (John 17:3). Without it, there is no life. It is here that the Lord himself complains in Hosea 4:6, "My people are perished for lack of knowledge." And so, it comes to pass, that many receive this sacrament without any benefit to themselves, because they are not able to discern it correctly. We should therefore all our life long carefully exercise ourselves in the word of God, so that, when we shall come to examine ourselves concerning our knowledge, we may the more easily, and with the greater comfort, try our fitness in this respect; whether we have attained to a competent measure of knowledge in the grounds of religion or not. In order to better ourselves in this, we are to make a trial of a twofold knowledge, which we ought to have: the one concerning God, the other concerning man.

Concerning God, we are to know that there is but one, only wise, and true God, subsisting in three persons; the Father begetting the Son; the Son begotten of the Father; and the Holy Spirit proceeding from both. This is a mystery far exceeding our understanding, yet so far are we to know and believe it, as God has revealed it in his word. And, therefore, first are we to examine ourselves concerning this knowledge.

Concerning man, we are to know that he was first created in uprightness according to the image of God, (Gen. 1:27). But afterwards, he fell through disobedience, and was again recovered by the meritorious death of Christ Jesus. This we are to examine according to the two parts of the word of God, the Law and the Gospel.

In the first, the law, we shall plainly see what we are in ourselves, even wretched and miserable sinners, corrupt children of disobedient parents; and that we

Chapter 6: The Examination of Our Knowledge

have justly deserved death as a due reward for our manifold sins both original and actual. We are carnal, sold under sin, and by nature the children of wrath, (Eph. 2:3).

In the second we shall understand what we are in Christ; and what that covenant is, which God has made to man in him for pardoning of their sins which return to him by repentance, and apply the same to themselves by faith. So that here we are to know two things: 1. The means of our redemption and reconciliation, which is the death of Christ. Christ, God in love sent into the world, to redeem them that were under the law, that we might receive the adoption of sons, (Gal. 4:5). Christ has delivered us from the power of darkness, (Col. 1:13).

2. The means, by which we may apply this to ourselves; namely faith; which is a gift of God, begotten and increased by hearing the word, and receiving the sacrament. Let us, therefore, seriously examine ourselves, whether we have learned out of the word of God our first innocence, which we had by creation. And that we have learned about our misery, which we fell into by transgression, as well as, the happiness which we have obtained again by our sweet and blessed redemption. For in those things ought everyone to be instructed, which approaches the Lord's table.

Besides this knowledge of God and man, we are further to have a particular knowledge of the sacrament itself; where we are to try, whether we rightly discern the elements from the Lord's body, and their true use. In this we must consider, that the bread and wine, (in themselves ordinary) being ordained of Christ, have now become holy. And where Christ blessed this sacrament at the first institution, we are to know that it is a blessed sacrament. This is because, whatever he blesses, is blessed; and that it will be a means of great blessing to us if rightly received. And where Christ gave the same after supper, we must further know, that it was not ordained to satisfy our bodily hunger. For, if any man in this way hungers, Paul tells him that he must eat at home, (1 Cor. 11:34). The supper was given for the refreshing of our wearied souls by the commemoration of Christ's death for us, and of our communion with him. But of this particular knowledge of the sacrament, we find this more in the beginning of the first chapter. In this, as in the former, we must diligently try and examine ourselves; for, except we know all these things, we are not to partake at the Lord's table; because without it, whatever we do, is but blind devotion.

Chapter 7:
The Examination of Our Repentance

So, now that we understand what we are to know by way of knowledge, which we ought to increase in, as for our *reconciliation*, we are to examine ourselves in those things which concern either God or our neighbors; because we have and do often offend both.

Those, which concern God, are principally two things. 1. Repentance by which we testify of our hearty sorrow for offending him, with a desire of amendment. 2. Faith, by which we take hold on his mercy, for their pardon and forgiveness.

First, we are to try whether we have attained to a competent measure of repentance. And indeed, if we truly look into ourselves, and consider that we must one day give an account for every idle word, we shall find enough matter for repentance, if our hearts are not hardened in sin. Now, that it is necessary to examine ourselves in this, appears from this, because without it we have no ground at all for any comfort in Christ Jesus. For, a person who is filled with his sins, is no more fit to receive Christ, than a glutted stomach its' food. And again, to them that are defiled, there is nothing pure, (Titus 1:15). That is, if through unbelief, they remain in their pollutions; but to the pure all things are pure. And if we cleanse our hands and purify our hearts and so draw near to God, he will draw near to us, (James 4:8). As many as walk according to this rule, peace be on them, (Gal. 6:16). Let us then search and try our ways and turn to the Lord, (Lam. 3:40). Let us put on David's resolution before we come to the Lord's table, "I will wash my hands in innocence, Oh Lord, and so will I go to thy altar, (Psalm 26:6). In this examination of our repentance we must have respect both to the time past and to come.

In respect of the time past, we are to perform three duties. 1. Carefully search our hearts to find out our own corruptions; that knowing them we may better avoid them which is most necessary to be done and that in the first place. This is because it is impossible that he should seek to go into the right way, which does not first see his error. And, in this way we must know that he which will not set his sins before him here to his conversion, shall have them set before him hereafter to his confusion. If we will need to cover and hide sins, let us in love and charity cover the sins of *others*. For, "love covereth a multitude of sin," (1 Peter 4:8). That is, it does not lay them open before men to their disgrace, who have committed them. This is something many do, who delight to hear other men's faults ripped up to break their heart, but cannot endure to hear of their own. We should not so much exclaim against other men's sins, but rather be humbled for our own. We should lay them fully open before ourselves, so that we may come to a more serious repentance for them. Which I think, we cannot but do (unless we have more than stony hearts) when we consider the torments which Christ suffered for our sins; and see our own misery, what we are in ourselves. For, this must necessarily drive us to God, as a desperate disease to the physician, It should make us utterly to accuse ourselves and say, Psalm 51:3, "I acknowledge my fault, and my sin is ever before me."

Now the chief means, which we can use to come to the knowledge of our sins, are these two. 1. A continual meditation in the word of God, in this (as in a mirror) we shall plainly see all our deformities. And, 2. A seasonable conference and conversation with such as are themselves touched with their sins, both which are excellent means. And, therefore, we ought sincerely to love the word of God, because it discovers our sins to us. We should diligently read, and exercise ourselves in it, so that we may come to its full knowledge. And it should also heartily effect and love those whom we see to be in this way affected. When we have in this way considered that we ought, and how we may discover our sins, let us examine ourselves whether we have done this in our life or not, giving thanks to God that he has at any time discovered such or such sins to us. If we find that we have not done this (as God knows, we are all too slack in this) let us seasonably repent of this neglect, and be sorry that we have not repented sooner for it. We ought to desire that God will be pleased more and more to show us our sins, that we may better forsake them and serve him, as we ought.

Having in this way unfolded our sins before our eyes, let us in the second place examine how in sorrow we have humbled ourselves to God for them; for this is that, even our sorrow, which must move God to compassion. We know that God is near to them that are of a contrite heart, and will save such as are of an humble spirit, (Psalm 34:18). And therefore David, being pressed down with the burden of his sins, comforted himself in this saying: "the sacrifice of God is a troubled spirit; a broken and a contrite heart, Oh God shalt thou not despise," (Psalm 51:17). Where on the contrary, if we do not have any true sorrow, if our souls are not wounded within us for our sins, we cannot expect that either we or our prayers should be accepted of God; or, that we shall with the sacrament receive any comfort to our souls if we do not come to it with sorrow for our former transgressions.

Now there is a twofold sorrow, 1. Servile; when we are sorry for our sins (as some servants are, when they have offended their masters) not because we have sinned against such a master, but because we have by it made ourselves subject to the punishment due to our offence. This is not that sorrow which God expects of us; for it rather drives us to despair, than to any pious meditations. But secondly, 2. A filial sorrow; when (like natural children) we grieve for our sins; not so much in respect of the punishment due to us, as that we have sinned against so merciful and loving a Father. This is that true sorrow, with which we ought to be affected.

Chapter 7: The Examination of Our Repentance

Which we may obtain in two ways. First, by ourselves. Secondly, by the help of others also.

By ourselves; and so, by the consideration especially of two things: first who it is that we have offended; even God himself, who in tender mercy towards us, gave his only begotten Son to die for our sins. The consideration of this cannot but work in us a true sorrow, that we should offend so merciful a God; for what son is there (if he has in him the affection of a son) but would grieve that he should offend a father, which has been ever loving and kind to him.

2. The grievousness of our sins, which we have committed; which will plainly appear, if we consider them either in respect of ourselves, how deadly they wound the conscience; or with reference to others, how infectious they have been to them; whom we have often drawn into the same faults, which we ourselves have committed; and so have made them guilty of our sins, and ourselves of theirs.

The next means, to attain this sorrow, is the help of other men, who are themselves touched with a feeling in this kind; with whom we ought to accompany ourselves, and patiently to accept of their admonitions, still accounting them our truest friends, which most faithfully and roundly put us in mind of our faults. The hypocrite may esteem such as desire in this way to express their love, busybodies or the like; but David's wish was that the righteous might smite him in a friendly way and reprove him, (Psalm 141:5). And whosoever is a sound hearted Christian will ever strive to make the best use of such, as he can. Let us, therefore, examine ourselves, whether we have made good use of those means or not. If we have not, we ought to humble ourselves before God for this neglect as well; earnestly beseeching him that he will work in us true sorrow for our past sins, with desire of amendment. To which that we may better move him, we are in the next place to lay open and confess our sins to God; which is the third thing required in our repentance.

Confession is so necessary, that without it we cannot expect any pardon at God's hands, but rather some judgement or other. Solomon says, "He, that covereth his sins, shall not prosper, but who so confessth and forsaketh them shall have mercy." And John persuades us to this by the mercies of God, saying, "if we confess our sins, he is faithful and just to forgive us our sins, and to cleanse us from all unrighteousness," (1 John 1:9).

Now in our confession we are to observe especially three things. First what we are to confess. Secondly to whom. Thirdly how.

As for the first, there is a twofold confession. 1. Of thankfulness, which David speaks in Psalm 89:1, "With my mouth will I ever be showing thy truth." And, "every day will I give thanks to thee and praise thy name," (Psa. 145:2). This we are also to practice daily according to his example. But this is not that confession which is so properly meant here in the matter of repentance. There is therefore another, called *confessio fraudis*, a confession of sin; and this we are to make, if we will truly repent. This ought to be, not only of some sins, but of *all* sins as far as we can call them to mind; and especially of those beloved and heart sins to which we are most addicted. Which, that we may better do, we ought daily to renew their memory in ourselves so that we may be better and able to faithfully confess them, as often as occasion requires.

2. We are to confess our sins, not to men or angels, but to God, who is the Supreme Judge of all. There is indeed a time when we may make confession before men; either in public, before a whole congregation by way of penance, being by the church to it commanded; or else in private. This is for either satisfaction, to our neighbor, whom we have wronged; or for consolation, to the minister, when our consciences are troubled. But that confession, which is a part of our repentance for our past sins against God, and in this we desire full pardon for the same, we are to make to God alone. For it is he who is offended, and he alone, that can forgive our sins.

3. Our confession must not only be of the heart, but of the mouth as well. God, who made both, expects to be honored by both; and as both have been unclean before him. They ought both to acknowledge the same, that he may cleanse and purify both them, and with them, the whole man.

Again, our confession must proceed from a twofold ground. 1. Hatred of sin because by it we dishonor God, and 2. Hope of mercy, which is that we aim at in our confession; and it must further be qualified with sincerity, with shame and sorrow that we have offended so gracious a God, unless in the end God rejects us as hypocritical. Let us from this time forth leave off censuring the faults of other men, and begin to aggravate our own; and especially before we presume to come to the supper of the Lord. Let us take some time to ourselves, in this we may be most private; and shut ourselves up in our closets, and there humbly on our knees lay open before God those sins, which we have committed in our past life. And let us do this fully and faithfully, neither diminishing the number of them, nor mincing their heinousness, for God will not be mocked. These are things, which we are to perform in respect of the time past. As for the time to come, we must know, that he which will truly repent, must not only turn from evil, but also turn to good; and therefore, having confessed our sins past with sorrow for them, we must (if we expect pardon) constantly purpose forever after, by God's grace, to amend and reform our lives. We are to resolve (as much as in us lies) to avoid all occasions, which may draw us into the same sins again, and to make better use of those means which God has afforded us, than we have done before. We should do this so much more, by how much we have offended so gracious a Father. But of this resolution of amendment, we will consider this more in chapter 12.

Chapter 8:
The Examination of Our Faith

The examination of our faith, is that which Paul exhorts the Corinthians, saying, "examine yourselves, whether you be in the faith or not," (2 Cor. 13:5). The necessity of this appears even from this, that without faith we cannot please God in anything we do, (Heb. 11:26), much less in this weighty business. Yes, faith is so necessary that without it we receive nothing at all, when we receive the sacrament. Although with our bodily hands we receive the bread and wine, yet, if we do not have faith, we lack a hand to receive the body and blood of Christ, and the comfort which from there arises to our souls. For how can we be persuaded in our consciences, that our receiving is acceptable to God, and that the merits of Christ Jesus belong to us without faith? It is impossible that we should receive any more comfort than what we believe. And therefore, our Savior Christ says, "he that believeth on me, shall never thirst," (John 6:35). In this he implies that he which does not believe in him, shall forever thirst. Yes, which is fearful. In fact, "he which believeth not, shall be damned," (Mark 16:16).

Now, that faith which is here required of us, must not only be a general faith, by which we believe that the word of God is true, and that God is a just judge; (for this the devils themselves believe and tremble at it; and well they may, considering what is due to them; eternal condemnation) but we must go on further to a more special kind of faith; and (which they cannot do) apply the merits of Christ, and the promises of God made in it, to our souls and consciences. We should say with Job, in chapter 19:25, "I know that my redeemer liveth." In other words, I know, by the knowledge of faith, or, I believe. And he does not only believe in the redeemer of man, but that "my redeemer liveth."

Of which that we may more fully persuade ourselves, we must believe, first, concerning ourselves, that we are not able, of ourselves, to do anything that is acceptable and pleasing in the sight or God; for we have nothing but what we have received of God, as Paul testifies, whether a good gift, or ability of doing good.

2. Concerning the means of our salvation, we must believe, that the merits of Christ's death and passion are alone sufficient for our redemption, without any merits at all, or satisfaction of ours.

3. Concerning God, we ought to believe, that, if we truly repent us of our life past, constantly purposing to lead a new life hereafter, and sincerely use those good means, which he shall afford us, he will then be merciful to us in accepting our endeavors through the merits of Christ Jesus.

4. Concerning the sacrament, we ought to believe; that it is a means, ordained of God, to exhibit to us Christ Jesus with his merits, and a seal to confirm our faith. If, on consideration of these particulars, we can be in this way persuaded of our own insufficiency and unworthiness, and that yet notwithstanding on our

sincere humiliation and obedience, God will be merciful to us. If we cannot only say in general that God is a merciful Father, and that Christ died for the redemption of man, but every one of us in *particular* in this way apply it to himself, that "I believe that God is my merciful Father, and that Christ Jesus died to redeem me as well as any other," all this shall be plainly confirmed to such people in receiving this sacrament. In this, in this trust, God will in mercy accept you under Christ's merits. You must think, "though of myself I am unworthy," if (I say) we can find that we are not hypocritically, but sincerely; not verbally, but heartily, persuaded like this, then may we, having made peace with God by our faith and repentance, boldly approach to the Lord's table.

Chapter 9:
The Examination of Our Love

Having examined ourselves in those former duties towards God, we are to go on to another duty, which concerns our neighbor; namely, love or charity; which is a free forgiving of those that have offended us; with a testification of the same, when occasion is offered, and a reconciliation of ourselves to those, whom we also ourselves have wronged.

That we may be better persuaded to a due performance of this duty, we are to observe two things.

1. The motives to it.
2. The manner how it ought to be done.

The motives, which invite us to the necessity of it, are drawn from the consideration of these four things.

1. What we ourselves have done to others.
2. What harm we do to ourselves by not being in a state of charity.
3. What they are, with whom we are offended.
4. Where such wrongs, as we receive, primarily come.

As for the first, we are conscious to ourselves of a twofold offence, which we have committed.

1. Against other men; whom perhaps we have at some time or other more wronged, then they us, or at least our consciences can tell us, that we have been prone and ready to it, had we not been prevented. And how can he, which has been forward to wrong others,

make the most of every wrong offered by others to himself? We must here take notice of the advice of Solomon in another case, "Seek not," he says, "to have thy servant curse thee; for oftentimes thy heart knoweth, that thou thy self hast also cursed others," (Eccl. 7:22). So also, do not be hasty to aggravate the wrongs which others have done to you. For your heart can tell you that you have also wronged others.

2. If this consideration does not prevail with us, let us consider in the next place, that we have daily offended God far more than any man can offend us. And can any of us expect any mercy from God in the forgiveness of our debts, if we show none to others in passing by small matters of offence? Small I say, because the greatest are but small in respect of the offences, which we have committed against God. Our Savior Christ told his disciples plainly (and in them us) Mark 11:25, "If ye do not forgive others their trespasses, neither will your heavenly father forgive you your trespasses." This was verified in the parable of the cruel servant, who (because he had no compassion on his fellow servant, as his Lord had pity on him) was delivered to the tormentors, until he should pay all that was due. He said this with this application annexed to it, so "likewise shall my heavenly Father do also unto you, if ye from your hearts, forgive not everyone his brother their trespasses," (Matt. 18:34-35). The consideration of this, I think, is able to move any good hearted Christian to love his brethren, though they have offended him.

Chapter 9: The Examination of Our Love

The second motive to this duty is taken from the consideration of the harm, that otherwise we bring on our own souls, which indeed is greater than either we can do to others, or they to us.

This harm is twofold; 1. General; namely, a stain to all the good, which we have: for though we speak with the tongue of men and angels: though we have all other good gifts, as of prophesying, understanding of mysteries, *etc.* Yet, if we do not have charity, we are nothing, (1 Cor. 13:1-2). Let us not boast of our learning and other good parts, as long as we are without charity; for all is nothing without it, no more than a sounding brass or a tinkling cymbal.

2. Particularly, it is an hinderance, 1. to our prayers; 2. to rightly receiving the sacrament. The lack of charity is an hinderance to our prayers in a twofold respect.

1. Because, without love, we cannot expect to receive that which we pray for; for if we pray to God to forgive us of our trespasses, as we forgive them that trespass against us, how shall we hope that God will forgive us, if we do not forgive others, which is the condition of our prayers? To pray for the one, and not to perform the other, is to mock God in our prayers; or rather, miserably to deceive ourselves. For, "as many have not because they ask not: so many ask and receive not, because they ask amiss," (James 4:3). These are those who ask in this way without love. And who knows how soon they may stand in need of God's mercy?

2. It hinders our prayers in this respect; because without charity, we cannot join those, with whom we are at variance, with ourselves in our prayers. This is against the rule of our Savior, who bids us to pray, "Our Father ... and give *us* our bread," *etc.* We join others with ourselves in every petition. Now, how can we heartily pray in this way for them, whom we do not love? Our own consciences can sufficiently tell us that we cannot. Yes, and that we often have been faulty in this. Therefore, if we desire that our prayers should from this time forth be effectual, let us follow the counsel, which Peter gives to the husband and wife, 1 Peter 3:7, which is, "to live together according to knowledge, bearing one with another, that our prayers be not hindered." Which, if we do, our prayers shall be much furthered, as Christ himself says, "If two of you shall agree on earth, as touching the thing that they shall ask, it shall be done for them of my Father which is in heaven," (Matt. 18:19).

The lack of love is a hinderance to our due receiving of the sacrament. This is because the sacrament is a seal of our union and communion with Christ, so also among ourselves. As Paul says, 1 Cor. 10:16-17, "The cup of blessing which we bless, is it not the communion of the blood of Christ? The bread which we break, is it not the communion of the body of Christ? For we, being many, are one bread and one body, because we partake of one bread." So, unless we are joined together in love, we cannot be capable of those benefits, which otherwise would arise to our souls.

Again, love is the very badge by which we are known to be Christ's disciples. John 13:35, "By this shall all men know that ye are my disciples, if ye love one another." It is a part of that wedding garment, with which everyone ought to be clothed that comes to the Lord's table. Therefore, if we desire to be accepted when we come, and there to receive the benefits of Christ's death and passion, let us put on the bowels of mercy and compassion.

A third motive to this duty is taken from the consideration of the parties, with whom we are offended. They are men, yes, Christians, as well as we are. These are such for whom Christ died as well as for us. Shall we then think that it is hard to suffer some small wrong at their hands, for whom Christ thought it not too much to die? Can we persuade ourselves, that there is the love of God in us, if we hate them whom he so loved? Every one, which loves him that gave to them, loves him also that is begotten of him, (1 John 5:1). And whoever loves him that were redeemed, loves him also that is redeemed by him.

The fourth motive to this duty of love is taken from a serious consideration of the first origin, where these wrongs proceed, which we receive.

And here we may take notice both of the author, and also of the disposer of it. The first author is not so much the party from whom we receive the wrong; as much as he is the grand enemy of both us and them, who is the devil. He knows very well that a house divided against itself cannot stand; and so he strives by all means to set us at variance among ourselves, though sometimes on small occasions. He does this so that by it such will hinder us from the performance of good duties (as receiving the sacrament) which are the means of our salvation. He may more easily tempt us to worse employments, while others are better exercised. In this he makes his side stronger against us. And who knows what power it may please God to give him against us at such times? Therefore, as we love our own safety, let us seek to cross him, who in this way opposes us by his temptations. And if we will necessarily be at strife with someone, let it be with him, who will never be at quiet with us, until he has gotten the upper hand against us. In this we may more easily persuade ourselves to this duty, if we do not have respect so much to other men's wrongful actions, as to his wicked suggestions, which is really the cause of everything. We must assure ourselves, that, in putting up with a wrong, we right ourselves, and cross *him*, which should be our chief aim.

Again, the devil is the original author of our wrongs against us. So, God, who is the disposer of all things has a hand in it. He permits the devil in this way to provoke us. Perhaps it is for the trial of our constancy and patience, or for some other ends best known to himself. And, if we could but see that the finger of God is in our difficulties, we would patiently answer with David, Psalm 39:10, "I will become dumb, and open not my mouth, because it is thy doing," and so we would commit our cause to him, that he might make our righteousness clear, (Psalm 37:6).

These are the chief motives to persuade us to this duty of love and charity; to all which we may add another, taken from the exceeding love of God to us; who so loved us, without any love received first from us, that he sent his Son to be a propitiation for our sins, (1 John 4:10). Here the apostle gathers this powerful consequence, that if God so loved us, we ought also to love one another, (verse 11). We can better do this, and to see how, consider next, the manner how it ought to be performed.

Here we are to have respect both to the time past, and also to come. As for the time past, either we have wronged others, or they us. If we have wronged others, we ought to perform two things. 1. Undo that which we have done, by making restitution as far as in us lies. This is as according to the example of Zacchaeus in Luke 19:8 who was willing to restore four-fold whatever he had taken from any man by false accusation. Such ought we to do, and be ready to make something good, whatever we have taken from any man, and to give satisfaction for any wrong that we have done. Neither is it sufficient to be *willing* in this way to make satisfaction, when we are moved to it. But, we must also, in the second place, seek peace with those whom we have wronged, though we are not asked by them for such peace. This is the counsel of Christ himself, Matt. 5:23-24, "If thou bring thy gift to the altar, and there rememberest that thy brother hath something against thee, leave thy gift before the altar, and go thy way; first be reconciled to thy brother." He does not say, stay until; he comes to you, or, be reconciled when he comes. But he says, go to him. And so, David also advises us in Psalm 34:14, "Seek peace and ensue it," meaning do not stay until it is offered to, or required of you, but rather seek it. Perhaps those (whom we have offended) are far off, and we cannot come near them; or they might be near, and will not be reconciled to us; what shall we do in this case? Here we ought to use all means that we can to procure peace and quietness; but if either occasion or acceptance is denied to us, we do not need to doubt but that God will be pleased to accept our desire.

    Now, if others have wronged us, we must (though perhaps it may have seemed somewhat hard) freely forgive them. We are to love even those that hate us; where our Savior often admonishes us in every Gospel, saying, "if thy brother trespass against thee seven times a day, thou shalt forgive him," (Luke 17:4). And again, "I say unto you, love your enemies; bless them that curse you," (Matt. 5:44). But some may say, such a one has wronged me so much, that flesh and blood cannot bear it. It is true, if you consult with flesh and blood, it will seem hard to bear the least wrong. But, flesh is not a friend, whom we may safely consult. Rather, it is our bosom enemy whom we ought to resist. If we ask the counsel of Christ (whose counsel we ought and may most safely follow) he will bid us go and be reconciled. And Paul bids us to feed our enemies, and to overcome evil with good, (Rom. 11:21). And Solomon can tell us, that it is the glory of a man to pass over a transgression, (Prov. 19:11). As for revenge, it is not for us to meddle with it, because the Lord himself says in Deut. 32:35, "To me belongeth vengeance and recompence." And James will assure us, that to have bitter "envyings and strife in the heart, is wisdom which descendeth not from above; but is earthly, sensual, devilish: but that wisdom, which is from above, is easy to be intreated, and full of mercy," (James 3:17). Therefore let us grieve at such wrathful motions, assuring ourselves that it is a point of heavenly wisdom to forbear; and certainly, if we can but once find that God has worked in us a readiness to forgive those which have wronged us, and to pray for their conversion, we may esteem it an evident sign of sanctification.

As for the time to come, that we may the better preserve the bond of charity, we must resolve carefully to observe these two sorts of rules. 1. How we may keep peace with others. And, 2. How others may do the same with us.

As for the first, because others may outwardly wrong us either in word or deed, that we may in both avoid discontent and strife on it, we must propose to ourselves a twofold rule.

1. Concerning their words; which is the rule in Solomon, (Prov. 7:21). Namely, that we do not take heed to all words that are spoken. For this is that which often

stirs up strife among us, which otherwise might easily, and without any prejudice, be avoided. If men would not be too inquisitive and ready to take notice of everything that is spoken, it would be of help. And therefore, we should not here entertain but reject such men, who, under pretense of love to us, will whisper in our ears, and maliciously inform us against such or such a one. Solomon calls them "pick-thanks," or whisperers, talebearers; such as will separate chief friends, (Prov. 16:28). For an occasion of separation may be given (if it so taken) even between friends; as we often see that he, which is singularly affected to another, may hastily speak some reproachful words of him, and then perhaps he will presently be sorry for it. After, he may not speak the same again. Yet, this shall be enough to make a breach of love, if it is in the audience or a whisperer. Such people to this, (to speak the truth) is a mere incendiary, that will ever be adding fuel to the fire of contention. Where James calls the tongue "a fire," and "a world of iniquity, that setteth on fire the whole course of nature," (James 3:6). And Solomon says, that "without wood, the fire is quenched; and without a talebearer, strife ceaseth," (Prov. 26:20).

    The second rule, by which we may keep peace with others, is concerning other men's actions. This is that we take them (though sometimes wrongfully) that we be not easily provoked by them; for a hasty and furious discontentment on some small occasion, often breaks out to make a breach of love. Where, a seasonable deliberation would mitigate the matter, and so cover everything in silence. And therefore, Paul tells us, that love suffers long, and is not easily provoked, (1 Cor. 13:4-5). If we can but make true use of these two rules, we may easily, for our sake, live at peace with others.

Secondly, we must endeavor that others also by our carriage may do the same with us. To this purpose we must take away, first a common fault among us, which is a main cause of strife and enmity. And also, 2. Its occasion.

The fault itself is railing, scandalous and reproachful speaking. And this is so frequent, that few or none (if we look narrowly into our words) but are conscious to themselves of such things. It is so heinous in itself, that Paul ranks it with robbery and extortion, 1 Cor. 6:10, saying that neither "thieves, nor revilers, nor extortioners shall inherit the kingdom of God." It is also so pernicious to the sweet society of men, that it is that breath, which often blows the coals of contention so far, that they cannot be quenched again without blood. And daily experience teaches us that there is no such common cause of strife and debate, as scandalous terms which are so often heard among us. So that, if we can but avoid these, we shall take away the very ground on which our wrongful actions are built. Therefore James, beseeching us by the name of brethren, exhorts us not to speak evil one of another, (James 4:11). And Peter's advice is, that we lay aside all evil speaking, and, as new born babes "desire the sincere milk of the word," (1 Peter 2:1).

Now, that our speech of others may be such as it ought to be, let us follow the advice of Solomon, whose counsel is, that "it be friendly," (Prov. 18:24). A man that has friends, ought to show himself as friendly. Not uttering anything that may tend to their disgrace; that except by such discourtesies, he loses their good liking; but rather endeavor by fair, and courteous speeches, to knit their hearts faster to him.

Neither yet can we easily avoid this fault, unless in the second place we take away its occasion. By a tickling desire, that most men are affected with, to hear the faults of other men (though perhaps less than their own) laid open and spoken against is common. This quickly begets a suspicion of their worth, and on this we too readily build some calumnious report or other. If it shall happen at any time that we hear the slips and errors of another, we should not be delighted in it, but rather seek to cover them. For, "he that covereth a fault, seeketh love," (Prov. 17:9). He does not have the desire to see them laid open. This is what we ought to do, both for the restoring and preserving of love. In this we must necessarily examine ourselves before we come to partake of the Lord's Supper, and to be with others at the Lord's table. If on examination we find anything lacking, either that we are not in love with others, or others with us, let us according to these rules seek by all means to make good what is lacking, and then come.

Chapter 10:
Of Premeditation and Prayer

We have considered the first thing to be performed in our preparation, namely examination of our own fitness to receive the Supper. The second is the premeditation of the benefits, which we are to receive. These we must not omit, that we may better be stirred up to seek God, and to communicate at his table with joy and gladness. For there is nothing which makes us colder and backward in such duties than this, that we have not sufficiently tasted how good the Lord is to those which seek him. Only the consideration of this is able to move any man to a longing desire after him. Therefore, we must search into our own state by a serious examination. Otherwise we should yet fall back to a luke-warm carelessness of what we are to do, (to which the devil will be ever ready to tempt us) and so become the more unfit to communicate at the Lord's table. We become unfit either to God's glory or our own comfort. So, let us ever quicken our devotion with a seasonable premeditation *before* we come, of the benefits which we are to receive by coming. All which are comprehended in this one word, *life* which we receive in the Lord's Supper, by receiving Christ, who is "life itself," (John 14:6).

Now the life of a Christian is either the life of grace here, or glory hereafter.

The life of grace (which we obtain in this supper) consists of two things.

1. A happy freedom from a twofold evil, first of sin; from which we are freed by the death of Christ. It is by his blood (if we rely on him) that will make our sins (though as red as scarlet) to become as white as wool.

2. Of punishment, from which Christ has redeemed us by the shedding of his blood; so that there is no condemnation to those which are in Christ Jesus, (Rom. 8:1). Here we may boldly say, "who is he that condemneth? It is Christ that died; yea, rather that is risen again, who is even at the right hand of God, making intercession for us," (verse 34).

The second thing is a comfortable enjoyment of a threefold good.

1. An inseparable union both with Christ our Head, from whom nothing shall be able to separate us, (Rom. 8:38). As also with our brethren and fellow members in love and charity; which David accounted a good and joyful thing in Psalm 133:1-2. It is a blessed strengthening of our faith, of which this sacrament is a sure seal, as before said. Here, it shall come to pass, that we shall be able to resist the temptations of the devil, who strives by all means to make a shipwreck of our faith and us. We will be able to reply with David, Psalm 16:9, "I have set God always before me, for he is on my right hand, therefore shall I not fall." This is that which will make our hearts glad, and our flesh to rest in hope, as it is, (verse 10). Which brings in a third good, and that

not the least, that God promises to his people in this world, namely, *peace of conscience.*

Peace of conscience is that which we are most carefully to seek after, and which in the latter end, will be more worth to us, than ten thousand worlds of pleasure which we can enjoy. Therefore, David's counsel is, keep innocence, and take heed to the thing that is right, "for that shall bring a man peace at the last," (Psalm 37:38). Now in this how can we better keep innocence, than by being carefully and faithfully exercised in God's service? And what greater comfort of heart, and what greater peace of conscience can redound to a poor sinful soul, than the full assurance of the forgiveness of his sins, and his inseparable union with Christ Jesus which we receive, if we receive aright, by receiving the sacrament? This is that, besides which there is nothing in us that shall be able to strengthen and comfort us against our enemy the devil, in the day of our departure from this earth. Who will, then, be sure to affright us with the ugliness of our sins, though now in policy he covers them, so that he may, if it is possible, drive us to despair of God's mercy towards us. Then, I say, by the help of a good conscience, as Samuel resolutely spoke to the Israelites, 1 Sam. 12:3, saying, "behold, here I am; witness against me before the Lord and before his anointed; whose ox have I taken? Whom have I defrauded? And I will restore it you." So we will be able to surprise our calumniating enemy, and say, "Behold, Satan, here I am, witness against me before the

Lord, in this have I done those evil things which I should not have done? In this have I omitted those good duties which I should have done? When did I at any time despair of God's mercy, or neglect the same? When did I prophane, or abuse his holy Sabbaths? When did I condemn or neglect his word and sacraments? Here I am, witness against me. My conscience tells me to my comfort, that I have diligently, according to my power, performed what I ought, and therefore you have no part in me." If we can in this way clear ourselves, then we shall be able to say with Paul, 2 Tim. 4:7-8, "The time of my departure is at hand, I have fought a good fight, I have finished my course, I have kept the faith: and that which followeth hereupon, is, henceforth laid up for me a crown of righteousness." This crown is that benefit, which we shall receive, after this life of grace is ended, in the life of glory. In the meantime, while we live here, we shall receive, though not this crown actually, yet its full assurance, believing with Paul, that it is laid up for us, which the Lord, the righteous Judge, shall give us at the last day.

These are the benefits, which every true communicant receives at the Lord's table. Therefore, as we desire to receive these benefits, which pass all understanding, let us carefully meditate on them, that we may be inflamed with their desire.

But, because all that we can do, is nothing without God's blessing. we are in the next place to pray to God, that he will be pleased to bless our endeavors,

Chapter 10: Of Premeditation and Prayer

and to accept us in his Son; which is the third duty required of us in our preparation. Without the due performance of this, though otherwise we have diligently prepared ourselves, we cannot expect to receive any comfort of soul with the bread and wine. God alone gives such benefits to us, and he is debtor to no man. Let us, therefore, seek him by prayer for a blessing, who is the giver of all blessings. This we ought to do first in private, setting aside some convenient time where we may freely take ourselves to this duty. This should be done especially in the morning, when we are to receive the Supper. We should rise early and consider what we are to do that day, namely, sit at the Lord's table, and therefore, be sure that we consecrate ourselves to God by prayer and good meditations. Secondly, in public with the congregation, where we ought to present ourselves at the very beginning, so that we may join together in all things which we are to perform, and there at our first entrance pour forth to God as at all other times this or a similar prayer:

> Oh Lord strengthen me against the temptations of Satan who strives to draw away my heart from you, and accept the prayers which I shall now make to you through Jesus Christ our Lord. Amen.

Which when we have done this, join with the congregation in such prayers as are then used.

Attending the Lord's Table

In both we are to carefully consider two things.

1. For whom we ought to pray; and that is, not only for ourselves, but for others also, according to the counsel of James, James 4:16 "Pray one for another," which we learn from the pattern of prayer, the Lord's prayer, left to us by Christ himself.

2. How we ought to pray; and that is, first in humility, with a feeling of our own needs, for which the poor publican was rather justified than the proud pharisee for his vain boasting, (Luke 18:14). Secondly, in a settled and fervent devotion. When we pray, our minds ought not to be fixed on anything else, (as many God knows are) for God will have the whole heart or none of it.

3. In faith; with confidence that we shall receive what we ask; for he, "which wavers," that is, the one that does not believe, "let not that man think that he shall receive any thing of the Lord," (James 1:7). If we are deficient in any one of these conditions, we ask amiss, and so shall receive accordingly. Therefore, as we desire to receive benefit and comfort by the Lord's Supper, let us seek God for it. And as we hope to have our prayers heard, let us pray both for ourselves and others in true humility, fervency and devotion, and assured hope of obtaining.

Chapter 11:
Meditation at the Lord's Table

Having in this way fitted ourselves by the examination of our state, the state of premeditation of all the benefits, and prayer for a blessing, we may assure ourselves that we have prepared ourselves for receiving holy communion, though by reason of our weakness, not in that measure, yet in that right manner as we ought. And so, we have performed the first duty required of us, namely diligent preparation. On this we may boldly and cheerfully, otherwise not present ourselves to the Lord's table. Then, we are to be exercised in a second duty, namely, a seasonable meditation.

This meditation must be threefold: 1. Before. 2. In the time of the consecration. 3 After the same, or, in the time of receiving.

Before the consecration, when the minister is going towards the table, meditate on these two things. 1. Seeing the table spread, and the elements set on it, we are to consider, what place we have come to; namely, the table of the great King of heaven and earth. We therefore ought most carefully and reverently, to behave ourselves, both in body by a reverent and seemly gesture. Also, behave ourselves in our mind, laying aside all earthly thoughts no matter what they are. And that in a twofold respect, 1. Because the place itself is holy, and therefore ought not to be profaned by any unseemly behavior. These must be laid aside, as God commanded Moses,

Exod. 3:5, "Put off thy shoes from off thy feet, for the place whereon thou standest, is holy ground." 2. Because as the place is holy, so also God himself is there among us, as he says in Matthew 18:20, "Where two or three are gathered together in my name there am I in the midst of them." He is in the midst of us, beholding not only our outward gesture but our very hearts and affections; and ready both to reward those that honor him by reverencing; and to punish all such as dishonor him by profaning and abusing his holy ordinance. Which we shall do if our carriage is not with fear and reverence.

2. When we hear the minister say, draw near and take this sacrament, we must consider that God by his minister freely invites us to his table. So, let everyone lift up his heart by this or the like ejaculation:

> Lord, I am not worthy by reason of my sins to approach before you; but seeing it has pleased you in mercy to call me, behold, in humility and obedience I come.

Then join in prayer with the minister. In the time of the consecration we ought seriously to settle our minds on the elements, and the actions about them, for better stirring up of our devotion, and so meditate in this way:

1. When we hear the minister read the words of Christ's institution, and see him take the bread and wine, we ought joyfully and thankfully to meditate on the great love of God in setting apart his Son for the

redemption of us his enemies; which is represented in the taking of these elements, and setting them apart to be distributed to us, as seals and pledges of the same. Joyfully (I say) in respect of the benefit, which by this comes to us, and thankfully in respect of God's love, which is greater than all the hearts of men joined in one are able to express.

2. When we see the bread broken and the wine poured out, we ought to be exercised in a twofold meditation. 1). Of comfort; considering that the bread is broken and the wine poured out, not only to be more divisible to the communicants, but chiefly to represent to us the crucifying of Christ's body, and the shedding of his blood for our sins. For, he was "broken for our iniquities," (Isaiah 53:5). By which is not meant that any bone of him was broken, but that he was crucified. Where we should, every one of us, gather this comfort, saying to our souls:

> Christ Jesus was broken on the cross, and suffered an accursed death for me; by whose merits, I trust, that I shall escape the curse of that death, which is due for my sins to me.

Here, by the way, we may take notice how the papists err in delivering whole cakes to the communicants, which represent Christ *whole* not crucified, and so afford the less comfort.

2). Of sorrow, and that for our sins; the grievousness of which was such that they could not be satisfied for, without the precious blood of Christ Jesus. These were the spears that pierced him to the soul, that was that, which drew his precious blood from his side. And the consideration of this should breed in us a hearty sorrow, that we who are such vile wretches, as we are, should in this way wound so loving a Redeemer. And certainly if we do not grieve for those sins, for which he has so much pain, we may justly fear that the stupid earth, the hard rocks, and the dark graves, which trembled, rent, and opened at his death, shall one day rise up in judgement against us and condemn us. When, therefore, we see the bread broken *etc.,* let everyone in this way meditate:

> Oh vile wretch that I am, that I by my sins should in this way wound my merciful and loving Redeemer.

After the consecration, when the minister is receiving himself (considering that we are in the presence of God, who sees our very hearts) we should pour out our souls to him in this or the like declamation:

> Oh sweet Jesus, I do humbly acknowledge with the centurion that I am not worthy, that you should enter under my roof, much less to come and sup and dwell with me. But seeing it is your

> good pleasure to promise me this favor, cleanse me, I beseech you, from my sins, that I may entertain you in a pure and sanctified heart, strengthen my faith that I may fully rely on your mercy; comfort me with your blessed Spirit and so dwell with me forever. Grant this, Oh blessed Redeemer, for your mercy's sake, AMEN.

Again, before we receive, when the minister is coming to distribute, and offers the elements to us (considering that Christ with all his benefits is offered to us by God, as well as the elements by the minister) let everyone meditate in this way with himself:

> Christ, with the benefits of his death, now comes to sanctify and comfort my sinful soul, in full assurance of which I am to receive these signs and seals at the hand of his minister.

And so, as you stretch out your hand to receive these, lift up your soul in faith with this or the like ejaculation:

> Come, Lord Jesus to your humble servant, as my trust is you will.

This we are to do after the consecration, before we receive.

After this in the act of receiving we are to perform these two things.

1. While we eat the bread, everyone should meditate in this way:

> Blessed Jesus, I do heartily believe that you were crucified on the cross, and that for me as well as for any other, and, as I have now received this bread broken, by which my body shall be nourished. So, I believe that I have also received spiritually your body crucified with all its benefits; the full pardon of all my sins; and the strengthening and refreshing of my sinful soul; this I believe, Lord, help my unbelief for your mercy's sake. AMEN.

2. When we drink the wine, and while we feel it in our stomach, we should in this way meditate:

> Most blessed Redeemer, I do truly believe that your blood was shed out of your body, as verily as I have received this wine apart from the bread; and that for the remission of my sins, as well as any others. And I do also believe that with this wine I have received thy precious blood, by which my sins are fully washed away and my soul purified. And that according to your promise, I shall never hunger nor thirst anymore; because with this bread and wine I have received your flesh, which is meat indeed, and your blood which is drink indeed; with which I humbly pray

you to cherish and nourish my poor soul, and to increase in me hearty love to these my fellow-members, who have now participated with me, so that we may serve you as we ought, and that nothing may be able to separate us from your love; which I humbly beseech you to grant for your mercy's sake. AMEN.

This is that, in which we ought to meditate in the time of receiving; which being duly performed, we ought in the next place to take notice of a religions practice of those things, which are to be observed afterwards in our life and conversation.

Chapter 12:
Of Practice

Those things which are to be observed afterwards in our life and conversation may be reduced to two heads: namely, such as we are to do, 1. In the church, and 2. At home.

In the church we must perform two duties.

1. Having ended the former meditations, each man ought in particular to give thanks to God for his mercy, in this or the like form:

> O Lord, I humbly bless your holy name, for that you have in mercy promises to accept me at this your table among the rest of your elect and chosen people; and that you have so graciously fed my languishing soul with the precious body and blood of Christ Jesus. I confess, Oh Lord, that I am not worthy of the least of your favors; but seeing it has pleased you in this way to have mercy upon me, give me grace. I humbly beseech you, to walk worthy of this your mercy in newness of life to the glory of your holy name, and the salvation of my sinful soul, even for your mercy's sake, AMEN.

2. After this every one ought to join with the congregation in prayer and thanksgiving, praising God for his goodness, and so depart lovingly together with

Chapter 12: Of Practice

joyful hearts that God has so graciously entertained us his unworthy servants.

After we have come home, we are further to take notice of two duties.

1. Meditation; meditating seriously what comfort we have received by being at the Lord's table. On which consideration, if we find any good motions in ourselves, any assurance of the forgiveness of our sins, we ought by all means to cherish the same by the comfortable remembrance of Christ's death and passion for us; and so much more lift up our thankful hearts to God for his mercy. This Paul sweetly exhorts the Colossians, saying, "as ye have received Christ Jesus the Lord, so walk ye in him; rooted and built up in him, and established in the faith, abounding in it with thanksgiving," (Col. 2:6-7). And this is that, which Solomon makes a true note of a righteous man; that he will ever be increasing those good gifts, which he has in him when he says, Proverbs 4:18, "The path of the just is as the shining light, that shineth more and more unto perfect day." When, therefore, we shall find a little faith, a little love in us (as, God knows, the best of us has little enough) let us desire to increase it, and to have our corruptions diminished; for these desires are a beginning of grace, and a sign of a heart well affected. And of this desire we cannot make a better trial, than by considering whether we long to receive again the next time; so that these good beginnings may be more perfected.

But if we do not find this comfort in us, let us search into ourselves, whether there is not some sin in us as yet unrepented of, and whether we came not so well prepared to the communion as we should. If this is so, then we ought to humble ourselves before God, with sorrow for our negligence. If we cannot see this in us, but that we came well prepared, then must we patiently wait on the Lord's leisure, and pray earnestly that he will give us the comfort of his Spirit, with full assurance that he will grant our request, when it shall be best for us.

The second duty, in this we must be exercised at home, is a resolution or constant purpose of leading a new life, of which Paul earnestly invites us in Romans 6:19, saying, "as you have yielded your members servants to uncleaness, and to iniquity, unto iniquity even so now yield your members servants to righteousness unto holiness," and why? "Because being made free from sin, and become servants unto God, we have our fruit (not unto sin, but) unto holiness." And verse 22, "Shall we then be made free from sin, and become the servants of God, and yet return unto sin again? God forbid." If we do so, we receive the grace of God in vain, which Paul implores the Corinthians to take heed of, (2 Cor. 6:1). Now, what is it but to receive the grace of God in vain, when, after we have escaped the pollutions of this world through the knowledge of our Lord and Savior Jesus Christ, we are again entangled with sin again? And, as the sow to the mire, we return to our former course of life again? Peter will assure us, that it had been better never to have known the way of righteousness, than, after we have known it, to turn from the holy commandment delivered to us, (2 Peter 2:21). And well were it, if this were duly considered of some, who think it is sufficient to live precisely that day, in which they receive, (though perhaps they can scarcely do that) and presently afterwards live as profanely and loosely as ever they did. We must know that God expects a daily reformation of those which present themselves at his table; and, if we do not duly consider it, we shall one day with fear and trembling acknowledge it, as Paul plainly tells the Hebrews saying, "If we sin willfully after we have received the knowledge of the truth, there remaineth no more sacrifice for sins, but a certain fearful looking for of judgement and fiery indignation," (Heb. 10:26-27).

Now that we may better lead a new life before God, we must consider that to the direction of a Christian life, three things are to be known of us.

1. What we are to pray for. 2. What we ought to believe. 3. What we are to do.

The first being rightly known, it affords us a perfect direction for our hope. The second for our faith; the third for our piety.

The first we have fully set down in the Lord's Prayer, composed by Christ himself as a most exact rule for all our prayers.

The second in the Creed, which contains the articles of our faith, contained in the doctrine of the apostles, called therefore the Apostle's Creed.

The third in the Ten Commandments, written by the finger of God himself, and revealed to us in his holy word to be our direction both for our holiness towards God and our charity towards our neighbors.

These three rules of our life (the Lord's Prayer, the Creed, and the Ten Commandments) are daily repeated of those of the meaner and more simple sort; but yet (God knows) not so well understood, as they should be, by diverse to whom God has given a greater measure of knowledge. Never did our land, yes almost every house, more freely abound with fruitful and comfortable expositions on these rules, than now they do; yet who looks so far into them, as to know by them the full extent of any of them? There are some few indeed (of which God increase their number) who make a conscionable use of those good means of salvation. Where others are well content, yes, with delight, and they desire to read ,and that on the best days, vain and idle discourses, which are so far from furthering us in the way of salvation, as that like tares they choke the word of God, and hinder its growth, as we too often see by our daily experience. There is indeed a time for all things; for pleasure, as well as profit. But shall we spend the best of our time, yes, as some do most miserably, the greatest part of our time in such vanities, and altogether neglect those good helps for our direction; esteeming them too plain and homely, or not pleasant enough for our witty inventions, and acute judgements? Let such know that they which in this way neglect their own good, are guilty to themselves of a twofold crime:

1. Of unnatural wrong to their own souls, in stopping their eyes from beholding the light of salvation, which otherwise would shine to them; dealing in this as injuriously with themselves, as papists do with their deceived laity; training them up in ignorance and blind devotion.

2. Of a twofold ingratitude: first towards those painful authors, which like fruitful lights have spent themselves for the directing of others; whose labors do well deserve to be accepted among us; and we shall prove ourselves but unthankful members of the church, in this we live, if we do not make that good use of those lights, for which they were intended.

Secondly, which is the greatest, we show ourselves unthankful towards God himself, who has in mercy raised up such means for helping our infirmities; of which others, better deserving than ourselves, have been destitute. Having therefore such helps so freely offered to us, let us, if we desire to live more righteously before God, use them more carefully than we have done. We should endeavor in the first place to know what is contained in each petition of the Lord's Prayer; so that, when we pray, we may know what that is for which we pray; and secondly, for our faith, to know the full extent of every article of it; so that we may truly understand what that is, which we confess we believe. And because both of these are little available, except our piety is such as it ought to be, let us especially be exercised in the commandments of God; that by them we may understand what we are commanded, and what is forbidden. These are the direct courses which every true hearted Christian ought to take, and which will one day prove truly comfortable, when others, vain and frivolous, deceive us.

But because our piety and religious behavior is the chief thing required on our part to the leading of a new life, let us further see what rules we may yet observe for its direction.

This piety of ours is seen in these two things. 1. Our words, and, 2. Our works and actions.

As for our words, we should follow the counsel of Paul to the Ephesians, which is, that we avoid in our talk, all filthiness, all foolish talking, and jesting which are not convenient, (Eph. 5:4). He gives a very good reason for it. 1 Cor. 15:33, because "evil communications corrupt good manners;" and that oftentimes both in the speaker and hearer. But some will say, "What? Must we never use any pleasant discourses? No jesting at all?" Yes, there is a time for that also; so it is according to the rule of Peter, such as God may by it be glorified, (1 Peter 4:11), otherwise we may not. We should stir up our minds to an honest cheerfulness by civil and modest jesting; but obscene and prophane, which Paul calls "filthiness, vain and idle," which he describes as foolish talking, and jesting, which is not convenient. This, I say, ought not to be once named among us as becomes saints. For by this both speaker and hearer are often stirred up to loose and vain gestures, or at least wise to conceive and think of them, and so God's name is much dishonored. It is miserable to observe how frequently such speeches do pass as a current under the assumed titles of merry discourses. But let us remember what our Savior Christ has said in Matthew 12:36-37. "But I say unto you, That every idle word that men shall speak, they shall give account thereof in the day of judgment. For by thy words thou shalt be justified, and by thy words thou shalt be condemned." If we must give an account of our words, shall we not then be careful of them? Must we answer for every idle word, and shall we fill up our discourses with blasphemies, with obscene and scurrilous jestings? If we must give an account of them, certainly these will lie heavy on us. Therefore, let us rather with David set a watch before our mouth, and bridle up our lips, that we do not offend in our tongue. Let us be careful that our words are such, as Solomon commends, Prov. 25:11, "Fitly spoken, which are like apples of gold in pictures of silver;" that is; such words, as contain wholesome matter, and are spoken in a comely and decent manner, are as acceptable and pleasant to the ear of a judicious hearer, as silver pictures, adorned with golden apples, are to the eye of the beholder.

    For our works, we must, as Paul counsels, walk as children of the light, ever proving what is acceptable to the Lord, (Eph. 5:8, 10), having our conversation honest among men, that they seeing our good works, may glorify God by them.

How to direct both our words and actions aright, we must chiefly observe these two things, 1. How to avoid that which is evil in both; 2. How to seek and obtain, that which is good.

To avoid that which is in evil, four rules are especially to be observed.

The first concerns the beginnings of evil; namely, that we watch and pray, according to our Savior's counsel and practice. Matthew 26:41, "Watch and pray, that ye enter not into temptation: the spirit indeed is willing, but the flesh is weak." That way we will not enter into temptation, and so be drawn away to sin against God. We are prone to it, and unable to avoid it. And if it goes so far that we are once tempted to sin, and feel in us any motion to it, we should endeavor to resist this temptation *in the beginning*, and reason in this way with ourselves:

> Did I not lately receive the sacrament of the Lord's Supper, where I had a full pardon of all my sins past sealed to me, and where I vowed and promised to lead a new life before God, how then can I do this thing, and break my promise with God? I have put off my coat of sin, and therefore I may not, I will not, put it on again.

In this way ought we to resist temptations at the first, unless they get the dominion over us.

The second rule concerns the occasions of evil, which we must necessarily avoid, if we desire to avoid the evil itself.

The occasions are diverse, but especially these two:

1. Idleness, from which proceed many, and these sometimes heinous and crying sins. To avoid this, we must be careful to employ ourselves diligently in that vocation, in this which God has placed us. Otherwise, the devil will be sure to take an occasion to tempt even the best of us. We see this in David, who was a man after God's own heart; and yet, when he was walking on the roof of his house (while Joab and the rest were in the battle) he was tempted to commit adultery with Bathsheba the wife of Uriah, (2 Sam. 11:2). And how many do we daily see drawn away to lasciviousness, drunkenness, and such vices by this occasion? Let us carefully exercise ourselves in our vocation, that the devil may not have an opportunity to set on us.

2. Bad company, than which, nothing almost is more forceable to draw us away to that which is evil. Let Joseph but live in Pharaoh's court, and he shall soon learn to swear by the life of Pharaoh, (Gen. 42:15). And if Israel abides in Shittim, the people will soon commit whoredom with the daughters of Moab, (Num. 25:1). Therefore, God commanded his people to go out of Babylon, lest they be partakers of her sins, (Rev. 18:4).

And often are we partakers of other men's sins by frequenting their society; yes, which is miserable to observe. Diverse people of ingenuous disposition and civil behavior, have by degrees been drawn away to looseness and riot, by associating themselves unfortunately with vain and dissolute persons. And we may in this observe the policy of our enemy the devil; who, when he finds any man well disposed of himself, and not ready to yield to others temptations will beset him if he can possibly with this snare, so that he may either by the wicked persuasions or bad examples of others, steal away his heart, and allure him to that which is evil. Which should be a forceable caveat to us, to make us heedful what company we fall into, and with whom we acquaint ourselves, and if we have any care of our souls. The counsel of Solomon is seasonable in this who advises us, 1. Concerning the examples of others, not to conform ourselves to them by walking in their ways, but to avoid and pass away, (Prov. 4:15). 2. Concerning their allurements, by no means to listen to them, "if sinners entice thee, consent thou not," (Prov. 1:10). If they say, "come let us take our pleasure in this or that sort, let us go to such a place, where we may freely do what we will," if they in this way draw you, do not walk in the way with them, refrain your foot from their paths. 3. As for familiarity with others, he advises us to make no friendship with an angry man, and with a furious man not to go. Why? Lest you learn his way, and get a snare to your soul, (Prov. 22:24-25). Will you avoid gaming, swearing, *etc.* Then shun that company in this those vices are practiced, or else you will rather increase them in yourself. But some will say, "such an one is my familiar friend, and shall I leave him? That will be taken unkindly; shall I get myself discredit, where I may avoid it?" Yes, if he is never so near to you, yet if he in his courses forsakes God, forsake him, lest God forsake you. Yes, you may in it show yourself a very friend to him in leaving him from his evil ways by forsaking him; for Paul says in 2 Thess. 3:14, "If any man obey not our word, note that man, and have no company with him, that he may be ashamed." It may be when he sees you leave him, he will begin to think of his bad life, and so be ashamed of it, and by degrees leave it. Therefore, leave bad company for their sakes also, as well as your own.

The third rule is, how we may restrain ourselves when we are about to undertake any sinful action. And that is, by setting before our eyes this caveat, *God sees.* His eyes are over everything, (Prov. 15:3). And therefore whatever we do, we should consider that we do it in his presence. If this is conscionably considered, it cannot but breed in us both reverence and watchfulness. It will breed reverence in respect of his majesty and watchfulness in respect of his all-seeing eye, that we do not offend him, who will spy out in us the least fault, even if it is secretly kept from the world.

Again, consider how merciful God has ever been to you in delivering you from this or that danger, from this or that sin, in this you might have necessarily have fallen, if he had not upheld you. Then answer the devil when he tempts you, as Joseph did his wicked mistress, "how can I do this wickedness, and sin against my God?" God has been thus and thus merciful to me, and shall I yet offend him and provoke him to anger? God forbid!

The fourth rule is for our direction, when we are fallen into any sin; which is this. When we are overtaken with any sin (as who is not every day) we should presently lament it, and not suffer it to go on any further, lest it come to *a custom*, and so stick fast in us. This is a difference which Solomon put between the righteous and the wicked. Prov. 24:16, "A just man, he says, falleth seven times and riseth up again, but the wicked shall fall into mischief." The just man, though he falls into any sin, rises again by repentance; but the wicked sinks deeper down, even to the pit of destruction.

These are the chief rules to be observed to avoid that which is evil.

The next thing, which we must look into, is, how we may obtain that which is good. Here we must principally observe these two things: 1. Make use of all occasions to it, and, 2. Make conscience of every good duty. As for the first, we must first, according to the example of Paul in Phil. 3:14, use all diligence that we may press on towards the mark, still endeavoring to be better and better. And when we find ourselves deficient in the performance of any good duty (as God knows we are in all) we should do the same again and endeavor to perform it more servantly and seriously so that we may come to a greater measure of goodness. Again, we should gladly embrace the company of good men, that by their example and advice we may be brought to a sense and feeling of those sins, which we commit. This is to count it a great blessing of God, if by it we at any time are crossed in those sins, to which we are most addicted; as gaming *etc.,* and ever esteem best of that company, not where our ears may be filled with profane jestings, or tickled with superfluous conceits. But where our corruptions may be most roundly reproved, esteeming *them* our best friends, that will most plainly and faithfully put us in mind of our errors which is the counsel of Paul to the Thessalonians, "I beseech you (he says in 1 Thess. 5:12-13) to know them which labor among you, and are over you in the Lord and admonish you; and to esteem them very highly in love for their work's sake." This may be our direction for esteeming both of our familiar friends and of our teachers; both which (if faithful) labor for our good in the Lord by admonishing us; and both by it deserve from us a true regard as a recompence of this their love. Therefore, if any man desire to be furthered in good duties, let him testify it by loving such men.

2. If we desire to obtain that which is good, we must be careful that we make conscience as of avoiding every evil, so of doing every good duty, no matter if it is so little. We should be endeavoring with Paul to have always a conscience void of offence toward God and men, (Acts 24:16). And laboring to keep, not only some

but all God's commandments, according to David's wish, Psalm 119:5-6, "Oh that my ways were made so direct, that I might keep thy statutes, so shall I not be confounded, while I have respect to all thy commandments." Let us not deceive ourselves in thinking it is sufficient, that we observe the sabbath, and that we do not offend God by swearing, stealing, or such like heinous offences; and yet in the meantime make no conscience of a lie for our jobs, or of vain and idle discourses for delight; for, if we in this way do this, it is certainly an argument of a bad heart.

But some perhaps will say, "if I in this way endeavor to carry myself in all things, if I now and then do not give a little way, I shall be accounted too precise, and curious in matters which I do not need." If this is the case, yet, be willing to undergo that censure; and esteem it safer to offend ungodly men by your good life, than a righteous God by your bad life. And though others account it too much preciseness, yet you should not do so; but rather consider that God commands us to keep his precepts diligently, (Psalm 119:4). And if diligently, then certainly there is nothing in his precepts superfluous; nothing, which we may do or not do, but every one, though of never so small a matter, is to be performed of us. Whoever, therefore, shall endeavor to his power to keep the commandments of God in everything, is so far from being too precise, that he does but what he is commanded.

Chapter 12: Of Practice

To these rules, for avoiding of evil and seeking of good, we may add one more, as the rule of all the rest, and of our whole life; and that is the word of God. This alone is able to direct us in the way to salvation, as David testifies in Psalm 119:9, "Wherewith shall a young man cleanse his way? Even by ruling himself after thy word." Therefore, let us carefully read, meditate and confer about this word, and often; accounting, as well we may, every day lost, in this if we do not learn something out of it; ever desiring more and more to be instructed in it, and account it a great blessing of God, that we have its use so freely to direct us in the way of salvation. Neither let any man think himself so learned, that he does not need any further instruction; for the best of us comes short of David, and yet he prayed still to be instructed in the word of the Lord; as we may see throughout the 119 Psalm. Again, if we did know more than we do, yet we are dull in the performance of what we know; and therefore, we have need to read the same again and again, to stir us up to a daily practice of it. But that we may so use the word of God, as that it may be to us the *savor of life unto life,* let us at all times, when we are about to read it, lift up our hearts to God by prayer, that he may give a blessing to our endeavors; without which whatever we do in this or any other thing, it will be so far from being profitable to us, as that it will rather prove our ruin in the end.

He, which shall in this way set his heart to serve the Lord by denying ungodliness and worldly lusts, by living honestly, righteously and soberly in this present world; he, which shall in this way carefully receive the sacrament in a right manner, and hear the word with diligence, devoting himself to God by prayer in all things, which he does; he which shall in this way make conscience of his ways in everything; the blessing of God rest upon him, as it necessarily must; and that peace of conscience, which no man knows but he that enjoys, ever attend him here, and everlasting peace and happiness crown him hereafter. AMEN.

FINIS.

Other Helpful Books in Light of the Lord's Supper Published by Puritan Publications

A Treatise on the Lord's Supper
by Henry Smith (1550–1591)
How well do you know the doctrine of the Lord' Supper? Is your view the historic Christian view? Or, have your turned it into a memorial, or worse, hold to transubstantiation? Henry Smith practically and concisely explains the Lord's Supper for Today's Christian.

Gospel Worship, or, The Right Manner of Sanctifying the name of God in General, in Hearing the Word, Receiving the Lord's Supper, and Prayer
by Jeremiah Burroughs (1599-1646)
This classic work by Burroughs deals with the Regulative Principle: God alone determines the manner in which sinners approach him. This is a life-transforming and Christ-glorifying biblical work.

The Holy Eucharist, or, the Mystery of the Lord's Supper Briefly Explained
by Thomas Watson (1620-1686)

This rare work by Thomas Watson is a gem! The Lord's Supper is one of the most misunderstood "mysteries" in the Bible. Watson, simply yet powerfully, explains the holy Eucharist (the holy means of thanksgiving) that Christians have in relationship to Christ's work and death.

The Guard of the Tree of Life, a Discourse on the Sacraments
by Samuel Bolton (1606-1654)

When you participate in any ordinance of God, you draw near to him, or you offend him. Samuel Bolton shows that drawing near to God should be a solemn and holy act each time the Christian partakes of the sacrament of the Lord's Supper. A rare treatise by a Westminster Divine.

A Discourse on Self-Examination
by Nathaniel Vincent (1639-1697)

There are, among Puritans, "best" works written on various subjects. On the doctrine of self-examination, this may very well be the best extra-biblical work written. Vincent biblically and exegetically deals with the practical nature of self-examination for the Christian, and how the Christian is distinguished from the heathen.

www.ingramcontent.com/pod-product-compliance
Lightning Source LLC
Chambersburg PA
CBHW070206100426
42743CB00013B/3069